Discovering
Wisdom

When We Realize We Are Love

Everything Shifts

Discovering Wisdom

When We Realize We Are Love

Everything Shifts

Ann Ranson

Published by Ann Ranson

2014

Published by:

Ann Ranson
Waynesville, NC 28785
ann.ranson.author@gmail.com

Dedication

I dedicate this book to my father

Joseph Aubrey Ranson

1910 - 1984

Wherever you are, Daddy, Thank You

CONTENTS

Discovering Wisdom
When We Realize We Are Love - Everything Shifts

Preface

My intention in writing this book is to simplify wisdom in a way that will help you on your journey - your hero's journey, as Joseph Campbell named it. I'm most likely in the last third of my life - so have walked down a few paths and fell in a few holes in the road - lots of them more than once. Maybe what I've learned along the way can help you.

I have been discovering wisdom pretty much my whole life. Neither of my parents finished high school - so, not educated people. Looking back, they and many of my other relatives were some of the wisest people I have ever known.

I immersed myself in book learnin' - always seeking to understand something - anything. It's as though the world never made any sense to me. Social norms, society's rules, religion's faith, wars, psychology, the occult - I studied and studied and studied. I even got to the point where I understood most of it. At least at some level. And, yet, it all still didn't make any real sense.

I felt for years - still do most of the time - I'm working a life puzzle. With this puzzle my first job is to find the pieces. I know I don't have all the pieces. And, yet, I'm always trying to put the puzzle together. I very much want to see the whole picture. So, I keep looking for more pieces.

That's what this book is all about. I hope reading it gives you a few pieces for your own puzzle, as you journey through this lifetime.

I've studied a variety of subjects, so this work doesn't really have an overall theme - more an eclectic mix of wisdom I've come across from lots of different sources. Some of the articles are my original thoughts and ideas - some from people I admire. I'll always let you know the difference.

What you read here is not right or wrong. It is simply my opinion and sometimes the opinion of others. I offer these opinions as "grist for the mill" - as Ram Dass so aptly says. Grist for *your* mill. Take what feels right and leave the rest.

Like authors and storytellers across the ages, this book reflects the pieces I've been able to put together at this point in my life. I can't see the whole picture yet. I wonder if I ever will? I do know I will continue my journey - isn't that really what being alive in this dimension is all about? Discovery. And, love. And, peace.

I believe we are a global people hungry for peace and understanding. Lots of the old models have either out lived their usefulness in our time or are completely misunderstood. Life is easy, joyful and filled with love.

I believe love is more powerful than fear and when we realize we *are* love - everything shifts. I believe personal freedom and peace on earth are a by-product of being love.

Welcome to my corner of the world.

Ann Ranson, 2014

Discovering Wisdom
When We Realize We Are Love - Everything Shifts

Introduction

A new take on religion, science, psychology, relationships, success and many other cornerstones of the lives of most people. And, ancient wisdom. Ancient wisdom keeps getting repackaged - new and improved. This book will help you understand the seeds of wisdom from which many ideas have grown. Plant your own seeds - tend your own garden. No need to buy prepackaged wisdom. Here you'll learn how.

I have been writing a blog, discoveringwisdom.com, for the past year. This book contains the most read posts from my blog. If you don't want to buy the book, just go to the blog and read for free. I decided to publish the book since I want to reach people who don't read blogs or who may want to read the same wisdom in a more organized format.

A note here on why I don't capitalize "god." The word god has come to mean so many different things. People fight wars and kill each other over the various definitions of this one simple word. It's my way of reminding you to go inside, discover for yourself what the transcendent means to you.

Here you will explore the differences in spirituality and religion; psychology and common sense; science and science fiction; and, the unseen, hidden, occult.

Many religions teach their way is the only path to god. Not so. Just plain, flat out wrong. There are as many paths to god as there are human beings who have ever lived, are living or will ever live. It's personal. Not institutional.

A rudimentary understanding of psychology and good old common sense helps us live in this material world a happier, more sane being. A few basic concepts and you will be amazed how easy life may become.

Some scientists have gotten out of the box and discovered different ways to view our world. Orthodox scientists consider some of this work akin to science fiction. It's not. Science is also running into spirit! We live in a magical, mysterious world. Our logical minds keep attempting to trivialize it all. To fit the unseen into the seen.

Is the occult - the unseen, hidden, secret, paranormal - real? Well, maybe? Many of us are interested in the occult. We yearn for an understanding of a deeper, spiritual reality. Astrology, shamanism, ancient oracles all reveal the mystery we live in everyday. Until we can explain or see something we label it as out there, new age nonsense, woo-woo. Like electricity, once it can be explained it fits into our material view of the world.

Always remember electricity and magnetism. We have absolutely no idea what they *are*.

Reading this book will shake up your world. It presents a new way to think about what it means to be alive at this most exciting time. Some of the old models have outlived their usefulness. Are you ready to shift - to see you *are* love?

Discovering Wisdom
When We Realize We Are Love - Everything Shifts

Spirituality or Religion?

Many roads home and we are all at some level looking for home. I was raised a fundamentalist Baptist and, as I grew older, decided that wasn't my path. Eastern teachings make sense to me and I've learned a lot from studying them. I expect each of you reading this book have your own version of god/universe/source or whatever word you like.

For me spirituality is a personal experience of the divine. It seems to me where we get into trouble is in trying to explain our personal experience to someone else. Or, in erroneously believing our experience is the only and truthful one. And, where we really get into trouble is when we don't have a personal experience of god.

Religions - all of them - are really philosophical teachings. At some point in the past, some person did have a transcendent experience. They attempted to share their experience - to talk about what is beyond words. It's in the explanation or the translations of the explanation where we get into trouble.

Many religions teach their way is the only path to god. Not so. Just plain, flat out wrong. There are as many paths to god as there are human beings who have ever lived, are living or will ever live. It's personal. Not institutional.

In this section are bits of wisdom I've found concerning this very controversial subject. Here is the wisdom that is true for me. If it makes sense to you - great. If not, I wish you a safe journey on your own path to the transcendent.

Religion or Spirituality?

"Religion is for people who're afraid of going to hell. Spirituality is for those who've already been there." - Vine Deloria, Jr. (1933 - 2005), an American Indian author, theologian, historian, and activist.

Religious and spiritual people are both looking for a path to god. How to define god becomes one of the first forks in the road.

Many religions see god as a being in heaven, a father image at times, both loving and vengeful. Religions have lots of rules to follow - each sect has its own rules and usually believes all other sects are wrong. The "my way or the highway" view. Most religions place emphasis on outer forms of worship - going to church or temple. Sin is a big deal. It's critical you understand every rule so you don't inadvertently screw up. Hell is always looming. Religion is about loving god and fearing and obeying god. To me the operative word in most religion is fear. Its why I dropped out years ago. Not my personal path.

The spiritual view of god is very different. God is omniscient and omnipresent and can be felt as a living presence in our own heart. Spirituality says there is no separation between the creator and his creation. You are god, me, too. We discover god inside through love. We each find our own way - our own personal experience of god. And, on the way, many of us find ourselves in the hell of seeing ourselves clearly - the illusions drop away -

we stand naked and vulnerable. No rule book. Spirituality is not very concerned with a place to go to be spiritual - it's more a way of life - the shrine is inside. To a spiritual person there is only ignorance in the world, not sin. No judgment - only acceptance. A spiritual path leads to the feeling that all religions are valid - many roads home.

"The essence of religion: Fear God and obey God. The essence of spirituality: Love God and become another God." - Sri Chinmoy

Religion and spirituality do conjure up differences, but at the same time they are just two words. The boundary between religion and spirituality can be fluid. Rather than a debate between religion and spirituality, it might be helpful to remember they are both a path to god. Both paths can be walked well or not so well - it all comes back to us and our choices.

All Religions Are True, But None Are Literal

Joseph Campbell (1904 - 1987) was a teacher of comparative mythology and comparative religion - a true scholar. Bill Moyers did a PBS series of interviews with him entitled *The Power of Myth* - it brought a lot of Campbell's ideas to the general public for the first time. "Follow Your Bliss" and the "Hero's Journey" were coined by Campbell. *Mythos* is a three-part documentary that consists of a series of lectures given by Campbell over the last six years of his life, as a summation of what he had learned about the human mythic impulse - what he called "the one great story of mankind." He wrote many books, the most famous of which is probably a four volume set entitled *The Masks of God*.

I've learned a lot by reading his books and watching *The Power of Myth, Mythos* and other interviews. He saw all religion as myth, not as fact. He concluded that all religions at their core have the same essential truth. And, they are all mythological - not literal. You can imagine the controversy surrounding his ideas.

Joseph Campbell taught that all the gods and goddesses, heroes and monsters, angels and demons, Jesus, Buddha, Allah, Yahweh, Yoda, etc. - all represent various aspects of the human psyche - the human heart - the human condition.

This means there is no bearded father God. There is no Heaven as a physical place. The virgin birth did not actually happen - it's the metaphor for the birth of compassion and spirit felt in the heart. The resurrection of Christ is a symbol for humans opening to their spiritual self. We die to the old and are resurrected to the new.

Demons, the devil, do not exist out there in the world - rather, in here - aspects of our own being. Born total and complete, lacking nothing. What do you choose?

The holy texts are not to be read literally. It's all story, myth, metaphor - a way for all humans to learn about our journey here. Reading the myths is like reading an instruction manual for life's journey written in code. Joe Campbell breaks the code for us.

Joe Campbell discovered the same mythological themes cross all cultures and all times. The reason is we are all humans, having a similar human experience. When read from the perspective of myth and symbol, the stories are always fresh, always contemporary, always meaningful to our lives today.

His books and interviews are filled with very detailed analyses of the myths. It is amazing how similar the details of the myths are and how well Joe Campbell brings them alive for us and convinces us we are reading the same story over and over again - the one great story.

Here are some quotes from Joe Campbell which resulted in "aha" moments for me. Hopefully, they will help you on your way:

". . . the whole sense of myth is finding the courage to follow the process. In order to have something new, something old has to be broken; and if you're too heavily fixed on the old, you're going to get stuck. That's what hell is: the place of people who could not yield their ego system to allow the grace of a transpersonal power to move them."

". . . if you understand the spiritual aspect of your religious tradition, it will encourage you to do that [get in touch with the deeper part of life.] But if you interpret it in terms of hard fact, it's going to hinder you."

"My favorite definition of religion is 'a misinterpretation of mythology.' And the misinterpretation consists precisely in attributing historical references to symbols which properly are spiritual in their reference. What a mythic image talks about is not something that happened somewhere or will happen somewhere at some time or other; it refers to what is now, and was yesterday, and will be tomorrow, and is forever."

"I taught a course at Sarah Lawrence College on comparative mythology for thirty-eight years. I taught young people of every available creed. More than fifty percent of my students from the New York area were Jewish; many were Christians – Protestant, Catholic; there were Mormons and Zoroastrians and Buddhists. There wasn't much of a problem with the Buddhists, but all the others were somewhat stuck in their provincial traditions.

"It was the simplest thing; all I did was to point out the parallels and identities all over the place. You see, when there is a motif – such as that of the virgin birth – which occurs in American Indian mythologies, in Greek mythology, and so on, it becomes obvious that the virgin birth could not have referred to a historical event. It's a spiritual event that's referred to – even in the Christian tradition. One after another, these motifs became spiritualized instead of historicized. And the interesting thing is that instead of the person losing her religion, she gained it. It became a religion instead of a misleading theory."

"There are very few cultures that don't have a Flood motif. That's a basic idea: the dissolution of the world which takes place every night when we go into the flood of our own unconscious. It's the analogue of the mythological Flood: at the end of the cycle, there's a flood. The American Indians have lots of Flood stories.

"There's no cosmic flood; the Flood motif is a mythological idea. The whole notion that all originates from water, and all is going back to water, gives you a cycle: out of water, back to water, out of water, back to water; and each new cosmic eon, each new world-age, is, as it were, a creation out of water and a dissolution into water. So it's a mythological motif. . . . a psychological flood, and when local floods occur they become identified with it."

"The thing about Jesus is not that he died and was resurrected, but that his death and resurrection must tell us something about our own spirit."

"I think it's [our literal interpretation] the result of a strong institutional emphasis in our religions in the West, and a fear of the mystical experience. In fact, the experience of the divine within you is regarded as blasphemy."

"That divinity which you seek outside, and which you first become aware of because you recognize it outside, is actually your inmost being. Now, it's not a nice thing to say, but *it's not good for institutions if people find that it's all within themselves.* So there may be some point there about our particular situation in the West where religious institutions have been able to dominate a society." [Emphasis added.]

"No matter what name we give it, the God we have is the one we're capable of having. That's something people don't realize. Simply because they're all saying the same name for God, that doesn't mean they have the same relationship to That, or the same concept of what It is. And the concept of God is only a foreground of the experience"

". . . the most difficult, *is the getting rid of your god to go to God.* Wow! That's the big adventure, isn't it? *That's the ultimate adventure.* That's what you have to strive for every minute of your life: to get rid of the life that you have planned in order to have the life that's waiting to be yours.

Discovering Wisdom
When We Realize We Are Love - Everything Shifts

Move. Move. Move into the Transcendent. That's the whole sense of the adventure, I think." [Emphasis added.]

". . . you really can't follow a guru. You can't ask somebody to give The Reason, but you can find one for yourself; you decide what the meaning of your life is to be. People talk about the meaning of life; there is no meaning of life - there are lots of meanings of different lives, and you must decide what you want your own to be."

Love

To most of us love is a verb - an action word - "I love you!" Or, we sometimes say we love certain music or maybe a favorite dessert. We talk about our love life - or lack of a love life. Sometimes we feel if we don't have another in our life "to love" or "to love us," then we aren't complete in some way. I need you to fulfill me.

It occurred to me a year or so ago that love is also a noun - "I *am* love!" Actually, I think until we each realize that we *are* love - it might be difficult to truly love another. Most of the philosophical teachings over time have taught this in some form. I've heard it described as your "ground of being." "God *is* love" was the mantra of the '60s. Some people feel that enlightenment is the realization that you are love. Right now. Nothing to do.

Marianne Williamson, when writing about *The Course in Miracles* says: "Our deepest fear is not that we are inadequate. Our deepest fear is that we are powerful beyond measure. It is our *light* not our darkness that most frightens us."

I wonder why we don't realize we *are* love - god, source, the universal energy - pick your favorite word - manifesting on this beautiful planet - bringing our own uniqueness to the human community? I don't have the answer to that question. I'd be interested to hear what you think.

I'll close with Rumi: "Your task is not to seek for love, but merely to seek and find all the barriers within yourself that you built against it."

Limitless Unconditional Love

Wow! Just take a minute to consider what that feels like. You are, you are surrounded by and you are merged with limitless unconditional love. Everywhere and everywhen. No need to try, to be something or someone you are not, no effort at all is required - you *are* love. You are cherished, eternal, are filled with limitless possibilities of what you can do and become. You are love. At the ground of our being, our lives are incredibly easy, filled with magic and wonder.

Consider how our lives in this material reality would be different if each of us realized this state of being. I am love - you, too - we are the same. And, unique - each with precious gifts to give. Differing points of view, differing beliefs - all reflecting our own lessons as we journey here. Wouldn't it be great if we could all go to school together and yet realize our oneness?

It is obviously easy for us to get off track. We have forgotten we are the same - at our core - all love. Instead we focus our conscious minds on difference - we even kill each other over our difference. Or, at the other end of the scale - we harm each other emotionally, psychologically. The insidious thing about our actions is they are mostly unconscious. The product of programming by well meaning care givers, teachers, religions, politics, society, the evening news, marketing.

So, what's the way out? The solution? What can each of us do to fill our world with peace and love? We can *change* - at our most fundamental way of relating. We can realize and *live* limitless unconditional love.

We're All Just Walking Each Other Home

The title of this post is one of my favorite quotes from Ram Dass. To me *home* is knowing we are love - clear seeing - ourselves, each other and our world. Our very active minds sort of put up lots of smoke screens, clouding reality. We easily revert to programming.

Did you ever have the experience of finding yourself in a situation and seriously not believing you were there? Almost like you hadn't been in your own life for a period of time and just woke up to a moment of clarity. I had a friend years ago who was married to a woman who drank a lot of alcohol - she was the life of the party who usually became the nightmare of the party before the evening ended. He decided to totally stop drinking. After a few months passed he and I were having lunch and he said, "I woke up one day and was shocked - I'm married to her?!" He honestly, after several years of marriage, just saw his wife with new found clarity.

So, there are lots of ways we get lost out here in this material world.

We can come *home* to the experience of love as a state of being. No self judgment or criticism. No trying to be something or somebody. No shoulds. No coulds. No effort at all. Simply resting in our hearts and in the knowing that we are each total and complete, lacking nothing. It's amazing how difficult we make life. The magic happens when we let go of trying to control our world - to make it fit some sort of imaginary program we have labeled as good. We can just simply let go into who we really are - total love.

As human beings, we are all in this together. However you want to define *this*. No true separation - only the illusion of separation. What I do, think, say and feel affects you. Literally. Same is true for you and all beings everywhere and everywhen.

I feel a change - a shift - I believe we are all waking up, looking around at each other and it's beginning to dawn on us that we are just walking each other home. Groovy!

Imagination

I'm beginning to see that it isn't the answers that are important - my answers yesterday are different than my answers tomorrow will be. What's important is the questioning - the imagining - the creating.

I am not even there in the imagining, the creating, really. Certainly not important in that process. I'm the vehicle of creating, asking. My purpose may be simply to imagine, ask, question, create - the act itself, in my own individual unique way, bringing into the world of form what was not there before. What's being created is real, but I have no attachment to it - I'm tripping out on creating.

Where do the ideas, the thoughts in my imagining come from?

The Seen is *Unreal* - The Unseen is *Real*

The following quote is taken from *Dynamic Thought* by Henry Thomas Hamblin, written in 1921:

"To the ordinary 'man in the street' a thought is an 'airy nothing' - a mere flash in the consciousness - it comes, it goes, and there is an end to it. To the student of Mind, however, thought is known to be the power that is greater than any other power - a force that controls all other forces. An American writer speaking of Universal Mind says:

'It thinks, and Suns spring into shape;

It wills, and Worlds disintegrate;

It loves and Souls are born.'

"It will thus be seen that thought is the origin of the visible Universe. All that we see around us is the result of thought. We may even go further, and say that all the invisible forces, which keep the wonderful machinery of the Universe working perfectly and smoothly, are but the thought-energies of the same Universal Mind.

"*As in the macrocosm so is it in the microcosm; the subliminal mind of man is the same in essence as the Universal Mind of the Universe; the difference is not one of kind but of degree.*

"In our world, our circumstances, our life, our bodies, we stand supreme, or rather we have within us the power, which properly directed, can make us supreme. This power is 'Thought.' Thought is so subtle, so elusive, that it has by the majority of men, been considered impossible of control, but the greatest philosophers, seers and leaders in the World's history have known differently. All that they achieved, they accomplished through the power of thought; and this was possible because they had learned the art of thought control." [Emphasis Added]

Thought encompasses our desires, feelings, emotions, beliefs, worldview - and, lots of other things you can add to the list. From our thoughts our world is created. Said another way - from the unseen (thoughts) the seen (material world) is created. This idea comes from Eastern teachings.

If we desire happiness, that desire is a thought. If we desire more money, more love, more fun - all thoughts. The question is which of our thoughts - what of our *unseen* world - will we choose to create in this material world - to bring it into the *seen*?

Henry Thomas Hamblin also says in the above quote: *"the subliminal mind of man is the same in essence as the Universal Mind of the Universe; the difference is not one of kind but of degree."* I'm sure you've heard the teachings that if we set intentions for what we want, we are more likely to attract that into our lives. Perhaps this is the mechanism through which that works? If my mind and the Universal Mind are the same essence, then it makes sense to me that my thoughts are heard - felt - at one with - or however you want to think of it - by the Universal Mind.

Ask yourself: Are my *seen* job, car, toys, home, relationships real? Or, do I simply *think* those things will bring me closer to what I truly desire, the *unseen* - love, peace, harmony, joy, happiness, fun - or whatever you seek within?

Think about it - only the *unseen* is *real*.

Magic Is No More Than A Change in Consciousness

Well, before we can change our consciousness, we have to understand what it is in the first place - right?

First, the psychologists tell us we have a conscious mind and a subconscious mind. Generally, we are aware of the material in our conscious mind and only partially aware of the material in our subconscious mind. This is *not* about those aspects of our makeup. The word "conscious" can get us off on the wrong path in a discussion like this one.

So, then what is consciousness in the bigger sense? Most people experience three states of consciousness - deep sleep, dreams and the everyday waking state of consciousness. When our brain activity is measured, there are clear differences in these three states.

It is possible to experience other states of consciousness - sometimes people refer to this as higher states of consciousness. Maybe they are just more complete states of consciousness?

The purpose of most spiritual practices is to take us beyond our everyday, conditioned, programmed mind into some of these more complete states.

The first shift or change is to become the observer of our life - most teachings liken this to soul consciousness. We become progressively less identified with our ego, mind and body and more identified with the part of us that is, was and always will be. As I said, some call this aspect soul - others name it the witness or the observer. One path to experience this shift or change is meditation - going into the stillness and experiencing the observer. As we move into this state, we find we are more intuitive and more centered in who we are - maybe calmer, finding it easier to cope with whatever life brings.

Next, we find we are living from this witness consciousness most of the time. Some traditions call this cosmic consciousness - the witness is experienced as unbounded by space or time while at the same time recognizing the body/mind is in this local place and time - in this material reality. In the Christian tradition the phrase "to be in the world and not of it" gets at this same idea.

In the third stage cosmic consciousness is experienced more fully. Here is where we experience limitless unconditional love - as a state of being. We know it's who we are. Our minds are free from the filter or the veil separating us from realms normally not available to us. We may experience extraordinary states or abilities - heightened intuition, clairvoyance, refined senses (taste, smell, touch, sight, hearing). We are tuned in to our life on a more subtle level. Dormant abilities are awakened.

Finally we arrive at unity consciousness where we have the experience of oneness with all that was, is or ever will be. The observer or the witness realizes oneness with pure consciousness. Observer and observed are one. Some would call this stage enlightenment . Here all life is seen as filled with miracle or magic. At last you are totally free from fear. Some call this a bliss state. You and god, the universe, source, creator, or whatever word you like - are one. There really isn't any separate "you" experienced at this stage.

It can be frightening to hear those words. "You" doesn't want to be lost. The thing to remember is "you" are an illusion to begin with. You made you up. Nothing is ever lost on the road to enlightenment. Simply one shift or change after another until the *real* world is experienced.

I believe the reason many people dismiss or choose not to follow this path is because it challenges our very foundation - at least here in the West. If we all achieved unity consciousness, what would change in your life? In our society? On our beautiful blue planet?

So, let's say you do want to follow this path. How do you do it? Enlightenment is not attained through reading or studying or through belief in something outside yourself - you are still at the level of mind in these activities.

It really comes down to regularly and systematically experiencing deeper states of yourself and integrating them into your everyday life. My path is one of daily meditation - going into the stillness - experiencing the witness/observer/soul and bringing that calm and peace into my daily life.

You may find a different path. The method isn't important. The ultimate experience is where the magic happens.

Stranger in a Strange Land

Stranger in a Strange Land was a 1961 science fiction novel written by Robert Heinlein. In 1962 it received the Hugo Award for Best Novel. I read it way back then and still enjoy reading it from time to time. It's a great book if you like science fiction, as I do.

The main character, Valentine Michael Smith, was orphaned on the planet Mars and was raised by Martians. Twenty years later he is brought to earth and the story goes from there.

Did you ever feel like you are a stranger in a strange land? I have - almost from my very first memory. I used to wonder what planet I came from and how I got dropped into my family. I was very different from pretty much everyone. I did and do yearn for a more peaceful world where people treat each other with sensitivity and love.

If you identify with this feeling, you may have found it difficult to accept yourself for who you are. Or, even to see yourself clearly. Always *trying* to be the person who would fit into or be accepted by your family or society.

As I have matured, I have come to embrace the human experience and have learned to not only accept who I am, but to celebrate who I am. At least, most of the time. Any of our early childhood wounds are deep and take some conscious effort to heal.

Also, if you identify with being a stranger in a strange land and if you like science fiction, you might consider reading the novel. It is somehow very affirming and very healing. Or, at least, it was for me.

We See the World *Not* As It is, But *As We Are*

This quote has been attributed to the Talmud and also to Anais Nin, neither have actually been confirmed. It's such fundamental wisdom I expect it goes back a very, very long way. Nothing new under the sun.

I have been studying astrology for a long time. It has helped me see myself more clearly and to accept myself as I am. Another great gift from astrology has been the realization that we are each just plain wired differently. I have studied the charts of and met with many people. Astrology is a very complex science - very difficult to learn. Each life and each chart has many, many energies at play. This next statement is a gross over simplification, but I'm going to use it to make a point. A person with an Aries Sun just does not see the world the same way a person with a Capricorn Sun does. I could use any two signs for illustration. As I said, we are just plain wired differently at a basic, energetic level.

Another factor in the way we see the world is our conditioning or programming. Family of origin, society, educational, religious or spiritual environment and economic circumstances all condition us. Have you ever truly left home? Do you know who you are - what you believe - what you want?

Ask yourself how much and to what extent you are programmed by TV marketing. Marketing professionals take pride in manipulating the general public into believing they *need* a product or service. These people are experts at *creating need* in their viewers. Apparently we are very easy to program.

There is no absolute truth. We each create our own truth, just like we create our own beliefs. And, whatever you believe to be true *is* true - *for you*! The problem comes when I believe my truth is the only truth. I am willing to fight wars and kill people because I'm so convinced that there is only one truth - mine. Or, I can't negotiate with a friend, boss, partner - I'm right, can't you see that? We are both right. Two views of the same world.

This real earth we live on is a magical place few of us can see.

We create an imaginary world for ourselves and then spend our lives pretending its real. If you see the world as filled with difficulty, anger, fear, sadness, scarcity, pain or lack of love - then you are filled with difficulty, anger, fear, sadness, scarcity, pain and lack of love. We see the world *not* as it is, but *as we are*.

So, what's the way out of this?

Well, first, you have to want to live your own life. Responsibility. The choice is ours to make. Do you choose an authentic, responsible, here's who I am, here's what I want kind of life or not? And, second, you have to have the courage to see the light, rather than hide in the dark.

The Field of All Possibilities

I was talking with a woman today who was blaming her husband, her parents, her children and many other circumstances outside of herself for her life. I suggested to her she is the Chooser in her life - she has chosen the life she has. And, through choice she can change whatever she wants.

A hard concept for some people to believe. Many people say they wouldn't have chosen the life they now have - so, it can't possibly work that way.   Tell those same people that they don't have free will and you'll likely have an animated discussion on your hands. So, we want it both ways. We want to believe we have free will and, yet, don't want to believe we have chosen the life we have. There is a serious disconnect in that logic.

The Field has many names. The name I like the most is The Field of All Possibilities. I know I'm crossing science, pseudo science and spirituality - it all sounds like the same thing to me, so I mix them all up very purposefully.

The Field of All Possibilities. The light and the dark. All things ever thought or done were choices between these two extremes - or, somewhere in between. If I'm the Chooser, why would I choose the dark? Some possibilities - I don't know who I am, so give my power of choice away to you and go your way; ego; greed; power; fear; apathy; laziness - you fill in the rest.

All wisdom teachings begin right here. You are a powerful being living in The Field of All Possibilities. You are the Chooser. God in drag. Source manifesting. And, you can replace those words with any you like. It's the meaning - the spirit of the idea that's important.

Peace on earth, clean air and water - we are all stewards of the earth - choosing with every thought and action. Accept that. Now what? One thing I know for sure, we can't change what we don't see clearly, accept and then consciously choose our future actions.

All possibilities - the sinner and the saint; love and fear; peace and war; compassion and control; truth and lies; joy and despair; happiness and sadness; abundance and scarcity; forgiveness and hatred. You see? All exist in The Field of All Possibilities. We humans have free will - we are the Choosers. This world we live in together and our individual corners of the world rest on choices - some collective - some individual.

What do you choose in this moment - and this one - and this one - and this one?

And, by the way, who are you?

Diamond Net of Indra

I recently saw an article on the web talking about the vast cosmic web of filaments that connect the galaxies in the universe. Due to some activity of a distant quasar the web has been illuminated so we are seeing it for the first time. Up to now it has been scientific theory.

Some call this web of filaments dark matter. Well, it turns out dark matter and dark energy are not dark, or matter, or energy. Those words could have been anything. Neil deGrasse Tyson says we could call them Fred and Wilma. He says the names - dark matter and dark energy - are unfortunate since they communicate properties that are unknown.

So what does all this new science have to do with the Diamond Net of Indra?

The Vedas are some of the oldest sacred texts, dating roughly to 1500 BC - 1000 BC. The metaphor - the story - of the Diamond Net of Indra came from some of these earliest texts. So the philosophical roots of Indra's net are deep and old.

The sutra describes a vast net that reaches infinitely in all directions. Through this net all phenomena are intimately connected - an interconnectedness of the universe or all universes. Indra's net has multifaceted jewels at each connection, each jewel reflecting all other jewels. Everything contains everything else. Through this interconnecting net all life is one.

Discovering Wisdom
When We Realize We Are Love - Everything Shifts

It seems people who lived a very long time ago had an uncannily accurate view of what our scientists have recently been able to see. They saw what we are now calling dark matter as an interconnecting net - a web showing us all life is one and that everything contains everything else. Ummm... I wonder what other scientific wonders we will *discover* that are described in ancient writings?

I also wonder how this discovery and others surely to follow will change our view of ourselves and our global community? Remember, *uni-verse* can be interpreted as *one song*. Now we have a *multi-verse - many songs?* We might want to concentrate on hearing and learning to sing and play the one song here sometime soon. It looks like the band might be warming up for a concert.

Listen To Your Own Truth

"The spiritual journey is individual, highly personal. It can't be organized or regulated. It isn't true that everyone should follow one path. Listen to your own truth." - Ram Dass

"Listen to your own truth." Great wisdom. First, you must discover what your own truth is. The reason that can at times be difficult is because we are so easily programmed to believe in a certain way. Sort out for yourself - how much of your truth is really the truth of your parents, your society or government, your religious orientation, your education, advertising, views of your friends or your spouse, and many other areas you can add.

You see, this first step takes a while. What is *my* truth? It's actually so very freeing when you realize you can think as you choose, speak as you choose and act as you choose - all consistent with your truth.

"It *isn't* true that everyone should follow one path." Wow! How would our world be different today if that one simple statement had been understood and honored over the ages that have come and gone? Or, if it was understood and honored in this age we now find ourselves in?

"The spiritual journey is individual, highly personal. It can't be organized or regulated." When I read a quote like this one, it just all makes so much sense to me. I find myself wondering where organized religion came from. And, a bigger mystery to me is how it has survived for so very long. I read statistics supporting the idea that people are leaving organized religion. To me that's a good thing.

Since the spiritual journey is highly personal I'm sure many find their path within some sort of organization. I'm happy for anyone who has genuinely found their truth and their path in this way. My point is - it's not for everyone - maybe not most.

Isn't it time we all live our *own* truth - isn't the most important thing to walk our own journey through this life unencumbered by dogma? Aren't we all mature adults courageous enough to realize we *are* - the universe, source, creator, god? Are we at a point in our evolution where we can let go of the need for someone else to tell us how to be spiritual? Where we can - "Listen to our own truth."

Yoda

One of my mentors is Yoda. I love this character. In 2007, Yoda was selected by *Empire* magazine as the 25th greatest movie character of all time. In my book he's closer to the 1st. Here is some Yoda wisdom to help you on your way:

Yoda: "To be Jedi is to face the truth, and choose. Give off light, or darkness, Padawan. Be a candle, or the night." ("Padawan" equates to apprentice or student.)

To me this is great wisdom. Let's begin with "face the truth, and choose." Face the truth - of who I am and who I am not. Of my life - the parts that are working and the parts that are not. Of my future and my past. Of the roles I play and how well I play them. Or, simply, of how I'm spending my time. Do, you see? Facing the truth. Rather than the constructed, illusion of truth. Time to "get real" as they used to say.

Lots of people don't want to face the truth because they feel they would have to change. Actually, you don't have to change. You may choose to change. But, you don't have to. The real issue is to face the truth so that you can then *choose*. Until you see the truth, you are not at choice. You are on auto pilot, running on programming and conditioning.

"Give off light, or darkness, Padawan. Be a candle, or the night." Now that I'm at choice, what's it gonna be? Light or darkness? The candle or the night? Love or Fear? Peace or War? Compassion or Control? Maturity or

Immaturity? Health or Illness? Happiness or Sadness? Stress or Balance? Forgiveness or Hatred?

Remember the field of all possibilities? Here it is again. Everything is possible. You are the chooser. Will you "be a candle, or the night?"

"[Luke:] I can't believe it. [Yoda:] That is why you fail."

The question then becomes - what do you believe? Do you believe you *are* love? Do you believe you are unique, beautiful, a shining light? Do you believe you are prosperous? Do you believe you are safe? Do you believe you are cool - with it? Do you believe you are smart, intelligent, savvy? Do you believe you have a calling in this lifetime? Do you believe you have unique gifts to give? Do you believe in magic? Do you believe in the field of all possibilities? Do you believe you need someone else to complete you? Do you believe you have to try in life? Do you believe in scarcity? Do you believe in abundance? Do you believe you are healthy? I could fill up a page with possible questions.

What do you believe?

Look around. Your life is a reflection of your beliefs. Your basic beliefs fuel all your thoughts, words and actions - they become your manifest life.

Can you believe it !?!

Yoda: "Train yourself to let go of everything you fear to lose."

Letting go of everything you fear to lose is a tall order. What is your list? What are you afraid to lose? Your job - home - car - money in the bank. Or, the love of your significant other - children - friends - parents. Maybe the loss of your freedom or beliefs you hold.

Why would Yoda advise a Jedi to let go of everything he fears to lose? Buddhist teaching says attachment can lead to suffering. Sort of sounds the same.

The objects of our attachments - the things we are afraid to lose - are transient - not permanent. Their loss is inevitable, thus suffering will necessarily follow unless we learn to let go of our deep *need* for them. We can enjoy our lives and at the same time recognize how changeable life can be. The Wheel of Time turns.

Letting go of everything means to let go of the fear you may have around losing material possessions, people, ideas, beliefs. Realize life is one large cycle of beginnings and endings. Learning to let go is a critical skill to develop as human beings negotiating our way through life.

It's not possible to hold onto what is already gone. How many times do you attempt to do that. Holding onto your youth, a relationship that no longer serves anybody, a job that doesn't bring you fulfillment, a life style you can't afford, a friend that depletes your energy - and, lots of other things you can add from your own life.

So, you may want to consider looking closely at your attachments and the wisdom of Yoda's words: "Train yourself to let go of everything you fear to lose."

Yoda had a lot more to say. Really pay attention the next time you decide to watch some of the *Star Wars* films. He is one wise character.

Life Is Uncertain - Eat Dessert First

This title is a quote is attributed to Ernestine Ulmer (1892 - 1987), a little known writer. I was talking with a good friend about the uncertainty of life and this quote came to mind.

We can easily live our lives believing we are in control. We're not. It's an illusion. An illusion we can spend a great deal of energy constructing and perpetuating. No matter - control is an illusion. I don't control you and you don't control me. I also don't control what's going to happen in my life in the next instant. Or, what's going to happen in the lives of the people I love.

We each have free will - we are Choosers. That's true. What's also true is - the universe, source, the creator, the field, destiny, our soul's path - brings us lessons to learn. We are the Choosers - our soul chose the lessons we are here to learn - sort of like signing up to take a class. Now, our ego sometimes puts up a defense against the lesson our soul has chosen as a learning. We may choose not to step into the learning that's before us - like not showing up for class or not studying for the test.

That might work for a while. The problem is the same lesson keeps presenting itself to us. In ever more intense ways. It's kind of like the universe is at first nudging us and then will ultimately kick us in the behind and stomp on us if that's what it takes to get our attention on any given lesson. So, we learn the lesson when its small or when its gigantic - we are the Chooser. And, we are the student.

"Life is uncertain - eat dessert first" means learn the lesson when its small - "the dessert" - the freedom that comes from becoming a little more aware - a little more conscious - about me and my choices and how I'm living my life. What's really important to me? Am I free or programmed? Am I doing what I want? Do I know what I want? Do I know who I am?

The uncertainty of life can be frightening or *invigorating*. How totally boring if we could predict everything that is going to happen in our lives. Let go of the illusion of control. Take a deep breath and see what *wants* to happen in your life. You may be surprised at how incredibly easy life is - "the dessert" is always right in front of us.

Everything is Energy

"Everything is energy and that's all there is to it. Match the frequency of the reality you want and you cannot help but get that reality. It can be no other way. This is not philosophy. This is physics." - Albert Einstein

"Match the frequency of the reality you want and you cannot help but get that reality." So, then, the question becomes where am I vibrating? Do I say I want love in my life and yet vibrate in a non-loving place? Do I say I want financial success and then think, talk and act in ways that are sure not to bring me financial success? Do I say I want good health and then eat and drink in non-healthy ways?

You see? "Everything is energy" means *everything*. Every thought, word and action. Sometimes it can feel like too much when you first hear that statement. "I don't have time to mind everything I think" one gal told me.

How do you see yourself, others and the world at large. Is your glass half empty, half full or over flowing? Do you choose love? Do you choose prosperity? You construct your world. Look around. What does the world you have constructed look like? Are the people in your life nourishing? How do you spend your time? When you look in the mirror, do you love the you that's looking back?

Once you choose to change your view of the world - then thoughts, words and actions sort of automatically line up with your new view. You begin to vibrate in a new place -

you begin to: "Match the frequency of the reality you want."

I Attract That Which I Am

The above is a quote from Deepak Chopra.

The movie, *The Secret*, made the law of attraction very popular. Like attracts like. The idea is a basic Buddhist concept - about 3,000 years old. Wisdom has staying power.

I've always had a problem with the way this concept is explained in the movie. It implies that we can all get rich quick, have houses in the Caribbean - anything our mind can conjure - all by thinking it, intending it. It also would have us believe the spiritual journey - the heroine/hero's journey - is a joy ride - no work required.

I believe setting intentions is very powerful. My problem with the way this is presented in the movie is my belief that materiality does not bring us lasting happiness, joy, peace, love. *Things* have the potential to give us a fleeting high. When the moment has passed, we are back to our inner selves - as we are. Quickly looking for the next material high.

"I attract that which *I am*" is a whole different message and one consistent with the basic Buddhist concept. To the extent I am love, I attract love into my life.

If you are an angry person, you will find anger all around you - your closest relationships and the most casual - store clerks, other drivers on the road, co-workers, you can add to the list. If you are a judgmental or critical person, you

Discovering Wisdom
When We Realize We Are Love - Everything Shifts

will see many flaws. If you are a fearful person, you will see threats all around. Some people in the US these days are getting permits to carry concealed weapons. Fear.

Who am I? It becomes an even bigger question when we realize who we are forms our entire world. Look around you. Who is staring back? Your significant other, boss, associates, children, friends, teachers, religious group, you fill in the rest. Every small and large thing you like and don't like about this group is a reflection of you. Listen when you praise them and when you criticize them. All you.

You leave relationships and form new ones as you claim more of yourself - as you change and see yourself in a new, clearer way. When you look at the other and know in your heart *you* are not looking back, it may be time to leave. My belief is its very healthy to let go of the past - it has the potential to keep us stuck in an old way of being.

Life is change. Again, a basic Buddhist teaching. Impermanence - nothing is permanent. Science tells us everything, including us, is in a state of perpetual motion. Either expanding or contracting.

"I attract that which I am" calls us to be open to new people, beliefs, experiences as we change and can see the "I am" inside in a new light.

I Realized I Was God

"I used to be an atheist until I realized I was god." - J. Krishnamurti

Jiddu Krishnamurti (1895 - 1986) was an Indian speaker and writer on philosophical and spiritual subjects. I came across him years ago when he and David Bohm (1917 - 1992), a famous theoretical physicist, held a series of conversations where they talked about consciousness and humanity. Fascinating stuff.

Krishnamurti taught the importance of self knowledge. He was opposed to gurus, religious teaching or any sort of societal conditioning. He said: "Leaders destroy followers and followers destroy leaders. You have to be your own teacher and your own disciple." Self-knowledge is an endless journey of discovery and totally unique to each being. I can't teach you your path anymore than you can teach me mine.

He felt we must all follow our own path of experience and thought - find our own truth. A famous quote attributed to him is: "Truth is a pathless land and you cannot approach it by any path whatsoever, by any religion, by any sect . . . . The moment you follow someone you cease to follow Truth."

When we identify ourselves with a group - religious, ethnic, gender, political - we are being violent because we are separating ourselves - holding ourselves apart. Ken Wilbur might say we are creating a boundary. And wherever we create a boundary there is a war. If we aspire to peace, we seek to understand and we don't belong to any group, we belong to humankind.

We carry with us the conditioning of our past and the past of humanity. Also, our own personal memories. If we let go of all this *past*, we are young again - we have a beginner's mind, fresh, open. Sometimes we have difficulty letting go of the past because we are afraid of the *known* coming to an end. We find our courage, leave home, embark on our hero's/heroine's journey and search for Truth.

Krishnamurti's Truth - he realized he was god. How about you? I wonder what Truth you will find on your journey.

Ladder, Climber, View

I like this concept I read about in one of Ken Wilber's books a long time ago. Imagine a stone wall that is too high for you to see over. Now imagine a ladder leaned up against the wall. As the adventure of life unfolds for us, we have new and different experiences. Some things work out the way we imagined, others not so much. We learn.

As we learn, we are climbing the ladder, one rung at a time. As we climb, our view of the world changes. So, while we are in any given era of our lives we see our world from the perspective of that place - that rung. We have in us all our experiences from the rungs before this one and yet we see the world in a new way from this place where we now stand. As our life unfolds - as we climb the ladder - we continue to see an expanded view of the world. Eventually, we can see over the wall - no boundaries - enlightenment.

Think back over your own life. I expect you see yourself, others, relationship and society very differently than you might have say five or ten years ago. Are you staying on any certain rung on the ladder of becoming or are you continuing to move to a new rung - a new view?

As we saw earlier, scientists say everything in the universe - including us - is either expanding or contracting. So, the question then becomes - are *you* expanding or contracting. You aren't staying the same. It's impossible.

Attempting to stay the same looks like this: clinging to the past; expecting a relationship to be the same as it was when it was new; continuing to treat your grown children like you did when they were young; trying to stay a child; or, "Trying to prove he still can" as the Jerry Lee Lewis song, *Middle Age Crazy*, says. You get the idea.

Ladder, Climber, View has taught me on any given day we are all on different rungs of the ladder. Obviously, we are each different climbers. It's no surprise then we each have a different view of life - of the world. So, rather than me trying to convince you of the rightness of my view or you trying to convince me of the rightness of your view, how about we each remember Ladder, Climber, View. We simply see the world differently. No right. No wrong.

Are You a Spiritual Being?

I count myself as a spiritual being - or, at least, a woman on the spiritual path. It took me years to really figure out what it meant to be "spiritual." I got lost in a lot of New Age practices and ideas - all good stuff - and, I learned a lot. But somehow not "it."

So here's my attempt at a definition of spirituality: A deep *experience* of my own spirit.

This experience is beyond our minds, beyond our thoughts. There are some clues you are living a more spiritual life - that you are getting there. Here are a few: love, joy, creativity, intuition, compassion, gratitude, a more quiet mind, a healthier body, a sincere delight in the success of others, a desire to help and a deep peace inside.

When I talk with other people on the spiritual path, it is such a joy - just the light shining through their eyes tells me we are swimming in the same energy, even if neither of us can find the words to express the experience.

So, why do so many humans not walk this path. What I'm about to say may be controversial, but it's my belief, so here goes. *It's work. And, it involves choices. And, we are back to responsibility.*

I have had to learn to see myself clearly - the parts I labeled "good" and the parts I labeled "bad." Accept and celebrate all of who I am - and, live *my* life. I've discovered meditation - again. The difference is now I actually meditate every day, rather than talking about meditating every day!

I expect all of you out there in the world have your own definition of the spiritual path, what it is and how you found it. I in no way mean to imply my ideas are right for you - many roads home.

I can't leave the discussion about spirituality without discussing religion. Those two words are so often confused. If my history is correct - all the major religions were founded on the teachings of a person who had a deep spiritual experience and attempted to teach others how to have the same experience. The problem is many people over time ended up worshiping the teacher - the person who had the spiritual experience - rather than seeking the experience for themselves.

I believe this comes from the Buddhist tradition and it sums the whole thing up for me. "My teaching is like a finger pointing to the moon. Don't confuse the finger with the moon." Wouldn't it be great if that sentence or something like it was printed as a footnote on the bottom of every page of every religious text?

I'll end with my favorite poet, Rumi: "You're not just a drop in the ocean, you're also the mighty ocean in the drop."

Courage

"It's not possible to be courageous if you are not afraid. Courage doesn't happen without fear; it happens in spite of fear. The word courage derives from *coeur*, the French for 'heart.' True courage happens only when we face our fear and choose to act anyway, out of love." - Julia Butterfly Hill

When you get right down to it, there are only two basic energies in the universe - love and fear. Lots of people over lots of millennia have come up with lots of names for these two basic energies.

Both are a part of our humanity. On any given day we all can experience love and fear. Sometimes consciously, sometimes not. I had a woman tell me she wasn't afraid of a damn thing! That spoke volumes. Maybe what she meant was she is aware of her fears, finds her courage and faces them? Or, maybe she is in total denial? Who knows?

Sometimes we are afraid of love. An old song asks the question: "How many times can a heart be broken before it refuses to mend?" We humans attempt to avoid pain - emotional, as well as physical pain. It takes courage to open our hearts and love one more time - and the next - and the next.

It seems to me one of the basic lessons here on this Earth is to learn to "face our fear and choose to act anyway, out of love."

The Power Of Now

"You are here to enable the divine purpose of the universe to unfold. That is how important you are!"

The Power of Now, A Guide To Spiritual Enlightenment by Eckhart Tolle is a very thought provoking book. I like his personal story and the wisdom he shares with us. The above quote from the book is a favorite of mine. Following is a very high level summary which will, hopefully, give you a taste of Tolle's view of the world. Consider reading his book - it is potentially life changing.

When Tolle was 29 years old he had an experience that brought him the knowing that is the foundation of this book. He was on the brink of ending his life - he had the thought "I cannot live with myself any longer." When he asked: "Am I one or two?" He realized there was an "I" and a "self" and that maybe only one of them was real.

You are not your mind. Our minds use us, we don't use them. We are the slaves of our minds. To be free we must observe our minds, our thoughts. Begin watching the thinker - be a witness to the voices in your head. Don't judge, just observe. Eventually you will come to experience that there is a voice and "I am" listening to it.

You can move beyond watching the thinker to realizing you can create a gap in the stream of thoughts by being in the Now - becoming intensely conscious of the present moment.

Emotion is the body's reaction to the mind. The more you are identified with the mind - the less present you are in the Now - the stronger the emotional charge will be. All emotions stem from fear or pain. The mind attempts to remove the pain - which it can't do because it is a part of the pain. Love and joy are glimpses of the gap - not emotions at all. They are states of being.

Consciousness: The way out of pain. Realize at a deep level that this moment is all you will ever have. Dwell in the Now. Pay visits to the past or future. Accept whatever the present moment contains.

Moving deeply into the Now. The problems of the mind cannot be solved at the level of the mind. The mind itself is not dysfunctional - it's a great tool. Dysfunction sets in when you become identified with it - to become trapped in time - the compulsion to live almost exclusively through memory (the past) and anticipation (the future). Time is an illusion - the more you focus on it - the more you miss the Now. Being in the Now is your only point of access to the timeless and formless realm of Being. The mind cannot understand this - only *you* can. Whenever you are able to observe your mind, you are no longer trapped in it.

To complain is always non-acceptance of what is. Leave the situation or accept it. All else is madness. Stress is caused by being "here" and wanting to be "there" - or, being in the present and wanting to be in the future. Die to the past every moment. You don't need it.

Egos are drawn to bigger egos. Darkness cannot recognize light. Only light can recognize light.

Don't get stuck on the level of words - a word is a means to an end - an abstraction.

Don't fight against your body. You are your body. The body that you can see and touch is only a thin illusory veil. Underneath it lies the invisible inner body, the doorway into Being, into Life Unmanifested.

Forgiveness is to offer no resistance to life - to allow life to live through you. The moment you truly forgive, you have reclaimed your power from the mind. The mind cannot forgive, only *you* can.

Enlightened relationships. They do not cause pain and unhappiness. They bring out the pain and unhappiness that is already in you. First you stop judging yourself, then you stop judging your partner - complete acceptance of your partner for who they are.

Love is a state of Being - it is deep within you. You cannot transform yourself, and you certainly cannot transform your partner or anybody else. All you can do is create a space for transformation to happen, for grace and love to enter.

Beyond happiness and unhappiness there is peace. When you are fully conscious, drama does not come into your life anymore. Ego is the unobserved mind that runs your life while you aren't watching. When you feel sorry for yourself, that's drama. So long as you are your mind what you fear most is awakening.

Do you choose unhappiness? If not, how did it arise. Who is keeping it alive? What is its purpose? When you are conscious, all negativity dissolves in the light of the Now.

If you can never accept what is - you can never accept anybody as they are, including you. Feel the emotional, mental energy behind your need to be right and make the other wrong. That's the egoic mind. Acknowledge it. Feel it. And, one day it will become conscious and disappear. You surrender. You become very simple. Very real. Surrender does not transform what is. It transforms *you*.

Personal Power

I first came across the idea of personal power many years ago while reading some of Carlos Castaneda's books. Castaneda (1925 - 1998) was a Peruvian-American author. He was a student of anthropology and wrote several books as the basis for his bachelor and doctoral degrees from UCLA. He wrote in the first person - describing the years of his shamanism apprenticeship with don Juan Matus, a Yaqui Indian from northern Mexico. His books were very popular and also controversial. I still re-read a couple of them every year or so.

His 11 books have sold more than 28 million copies in 17 languages. Critics have suggested that they are works of fiction; supporters claim the books are either true or at least valuable works of philosophy and descriptions of practices which enable an increased awareness. I've long since given up noticing what's fact and what's fiction. Fiction comes from imagination - a much richer world than the world of fact. So, what difference does it really make when you get right down to it? Wisdom is Wisdom.

Here are a couple quotes from *Journey To Ixtlan-The Lessons of Don Juan*:

"Power is a very weird affair. In order to have it and command it one must have power to begin with. It's possible, however, to store it, little by little, until one has enough to sustain oneself in a battle of power."

"Personal power is a feeling . . . something like being lucky. Or one may call it a mood."

"Hunting power is a peculiar event. . . . It first has to be an idea, then it has to be set up, step by step, and then, bingo! It happens."

"Trust your personal power. . . . That's all one has in this whole mysterious world."

I was thinking about personal power the other day and it occurred to me I am like a vessel. To the extent I know who I am, what I want, have found my courage, live authentically - we each have our own list - to that extent my vessel is filled with personal power. Maybe I'm completely filled, maybe only partially.

To the extent I am not filled with my own personal power - I have an empty space inside. The empty space inside sort of attracts the random energy out here in the world. Before I know it I can be filled with you, or an idea on the evening news, or an advertisement, or the opinion of a friend. You see, to the extent I'm not filled with and standing in my own power, I'm vulnerable.

I believe this is one of the mechanisms through which we lose ourselves. We have to have an empty space to begin with before it can be filled with something foreign to our being. And, when we are filled with our own power, we aren't tossed about by the opinions and beliefs of others.

If you are ready to explore the idea of personal power, you might want to check out *Journey to Ixtlan* - its way out there - helps me expand my worldview, that's for sure.

And, remember: "Trust your personal power. . . . That's all one has in this whole mysterious world."

The Balance of Power

I was talking with a friend the other day and we were discussing what we believe is a shift taking place in people around the globe. For a very, very long time our world has been governed almost exclusively by masculine energy. Really, more than just governed - masculine energy has set the tone, painted the worldview, influenced everything from science to religion.

Here in the US we elected a black man president for the first time a few years back. I voted for him and contributed to his campaign. His party selected him to run in the general election over a very qualified woman.

It seems many people in the US were ready for a black man as a leader but not a woman. I wonder why?

Recently Pope Francis said of gay priests: "If they accept the Lord and have goodwill, who am I to judge them? . . . They shouldn't be marginalized." He went on to reiterate the Roman Catholic Church's ban on women priests, saying the decision is "definitive" and "the Church has spoken and says no . . . that door is closed."

Clearly the Catholic church is ready for gay priests but not women priests. I wonder why?

So, you can see from the above examples *men* of color and *men* who are gay are being accepted. Good for them.

Discovering Wisdom
When We Realize We Are Love - Everything Shifts

In the leadership of the US and in the Vatican where is the balance of power to come from? The balance of feminine and masculine energies.

I've chosen these two examples, there are many others. I'm not attempting to make a political statement.

My question is simply: Where is the balance to come from? How will we ever live in a balanced world where decisions are made by equal representation of masculine and feminine energy?

And, yet, I sense there is a shift taking place. Inside each of us. Perhaps we each will realize oneness within - the union of opposites - the balance of feminine and masculine - yin and yang. Lots of the wisdom traditions teach this path.

Once we achieve that balance, individually - maybe that's when the balance of power will be achieved out here in the material world? I wonder.

Karma

There are lots of definitions for Karma: You reap what you sow. The law of cause and effect. If you want more of something, do that. I like "what you do is what you get."

Karma works - really, really well. The problem with Karma is we don't believe it. Or, we choose to live our lives as though we don't believe it.

If I want happiness, then I *choose* to express happiness in my life in all my interactions with others. Even when I'm alone, "don't worry, be happy" as the Bobby McFerrin song said. Or, if I want inner peace, I *choose* peace in all my thoughts, actions and words. If I want good health, then I *choose* a healthy life style. You get the picture.

Isn't it crazy we say we want good health and then work too much, stay in a state of constant stress, push our bodies too far, don't get enough rest, eat and drink in a non healthy way and lots of other examples you surely can identify in your own life. Then, illness happens. Or, we say we want a deep, loving, spiritual relationship and then constantly take our partner for granted, use them, project all sorts of our own stuff on to them, don't honor our commitments and all the other myriad ways we are pretty much harming them. Then, one day they are gone. So, we say we believe in Karma - what you do is what you get. And, then live our lives as though we don't believe in Karma at all.

We are each the *chooser* in our life. Karma rests on this principle.

Karma also has to do with past Karma. What have I done in the past that must be balanced out in the present. If you believe in past lives, what have I carried into this life from a past life that is to be balanced? Actions we label "good" and actions we label "bad" are both Karmic. We can and do bring good Karma forward, as well as bad.

Good Karma brings us ease in this moment, joy, happiness. Bad Karma, not so much. Sometimes we pay back our Karmic debts unconsciously - they are cleared and balanced out, whether or not we are consciously choosing. Any time you ask yourself: "What can I learn from this experience? How can I help others by learning this lesson?" you are balancing Karma. And, of course, meditation. Going into the gap or the stillness balances Karma. It's like going into cleansing waters where spirit, source, the universe shifts us in unnamable ways. Myths are filled with cleansing waters. Here the cleansing is in the stillness.

What do you want to get? Choose that!

I Control Nothing

We foolish humans have the illusion we control our lives. Life - the universe - spirit - god - pick your favorite word - gives me the lesson every few years that I control absolutely nothing. I guess I'm a slow learner. Or, I forget. Time to go back to school - again.

It goes like this. Something happens in my life I don't like. My thinking mind goes into overdrive. It presents me with lots of very viable options - ways to either escape from or deal with my dilemma. So, I go merrily along with the utmost confidence I am in control and making choices that are in my highest good. I see the light at the end of the tunnel or maybe I even think I'm out of the tunnel, back in the light of my happy, joyous life.

Wham! Here comes the unseen fast ball and it knocks me off my feet. Usually as I'm lying face down, angry or in fear, totally defeated, I see the absurdity of it all. It is at this point in my lesson where I laugh and cry at the same time. I totally surrender - give up - don't care - realize the whole thing isn't such a big deal anyway. And, I laugh and I laugh and I laugh at myself and the crazy illusion of control.

Next, I believe the universe says, OK you passed this test - again. The pressure of the problem dissipates almost instantly. The lesson: my ego gets a big time adjustment - my feet are more firmly on the ground - humility, gratitude and compassion are front and center in my life - thy will, not mine - OK, I get it.

Maybe I'm the only one in this particular life class? Somehow I doubt it.

I Believe In Miracles

"There are only two ways to live your life. One is as though nothing is a miracle. The other is as though everything is a miracle." - Albert Einstein

So, which way do you live your life?

We have been taught that miracles are unusual happenings and have been brought about by a special few people over time. Actually, that's not true.

Everything in life is a miracle. Some miraculous energy beats my heart and breathes me - you, too. That same miraculous energy allows us to walk and live comfortably on this earth - some call that miracle gravity. The list of everyday miracles is very, very long. As Einstein says: "everything is a miracle." I expect the reason he said this is because, as a scientist, he knew what is not known - only theorized. He came to the place where he saw the miracle.

How about other kinds of miracles? Experiences in the other than material world? Intuition, energy healing, psychic phenomenon and any other happenings that don't fit our normal view of reality? Are they miracles? Maybe they are abilities we all possess - parts of us that have become dormant - or not conscious. The Catholic Church, especially during the Inquisition, did a number on humanity. We haven't yet recovered. We haven't yet reclaimed our miraculous selves.

The truth is we know practically nothing about this world we live in - from a scientific perspective. And, yet, inside each of us we know everything. Once we choose to experience life *as* love, spirit, creator, source - or whatever word you like to name the unnamable - then we are consciously at one with the miracle that is our life.

Then we easily see "everything is a miracle."

You Are a Divine Being

"You are a divine being. You matter, you count. You come from realms of unimaginable power and light, and you will return to those realms." - Terence McKenna

Terence McKenna (1946 - 2000) was a writer and lecturer who advocated the exploration of altered states of mind by ingesting psychedelics. He died of brain cancer at an early age. You may or may not agree with his life style. He was noted for his knowledge which he claimed he acquired in altered states of consciousness.

So how does an old, tripped out hippie make it to my book? I look for wisdom pretty much everywhere. And, I mostly look for the same message coming from lots of different, unrelated sources. While in an altered state of consciousness Terence McKenna discovered he was a divine being - that we all are - a core message of all wisdom teachings. You are divine. Me, too.

"You come from realms of unimaginable power and light, and you will return to those realms." I was talking with a young girl recently. She has been taught to believe in the concept of heaven and hell - she asked me if I believed as she does. I explained I believe in love and in a divinity that is all goodness - there is no hell in my view.

Organized religion is based on fear - hell, in this case. It is the main reason years ago I chose another path. To associate fear, hell with god is just about as wrong as it gets.

Discovering Wisdom
When We Realize We Are Love - Everything Shifts

So, I agree with the tripped out hippie. "You are a divine being. You matter, you count. You come from realms of unimaginable power and light, and you will return to those realms."

Are You an Adult of God or a Child of God?

And, you can replace "god" with - the field, the universe, creator, true source, or any other word you like. Think about it. Are you a child of the universe or an adult of the universe? There's a big difference. In the West we have been taught for a long time we are children. No wonder many of us have a very difficult time maturing and becoming adults.

I believe there is a big shift going on inside all beings. A shift in beliefs. Science is supporting this shift - reluctantly - but, supporting nonetheless.

The problem with remaining a child is you never realize your uniqueness - your gifts - your joy - the peace and love that you are. We are always looking to something or someone outside ourselves to define us - to tell us we are good enough - to tell us what to think - how to act - what to believe.

Religion, politics, the health care system, pharmaceutical companies - all are based on the belief that we are all children who need "daddy" to take care of us. To tell us how to think, how to be healthy, how to find god, what's right and what's wrong. Maybe there was a time long, long ago when humans were inherently bad and needed "daddy" to tell them what to do? Who knows how this daddy/child thing got started? It's time for it to end.

Now - most people I know are far more in tune, in touch and saner than the institutions that are the cornerstone of

Discovering Wisdom
When We Realize We Are Love - Everything Shifts

society. I feel as though most - almost all - individual people living on this beautiful blue planet are really, really loving, kind, peaceful, mature adults - inside, if not outwardly. I believe we are approaching a paradigm shift - sort of a mass awakening.

We will always have the sector of people who are greedy, cruel, angry - *afraid*. Most of us are not afraid. Isn't it nuts that all our structures are geared to the few who are? And, those structures are also geared to keep us in a state of fear.

Now, why would that be? Why would our religious, political and health care systems want us to be afraid? If you think I'm wrong, check it out. Really listen to the commercials on TV - they are inventing drugs and bogus illnesses and then programming people to believe they feel a certain way - it's crazy. Listen to the politicians (if you dare) and the guy delivering the message in your place of worship. I'll guarantee you - if you listen with an open mind - you'll hear a lot about fear.

What if *"They"* (a possible new word for "god") - are wrong? Really, really, wrong. Elsewhere in this book I've written a lot on the power of beliefs and on the mind/body connection. And, the field of all possibilities.

Do you want to be programmed by *Them* or do you want to live your own life?

Just to be clear programming looks like this: You share the political beliefs of your parents or your crowd without having given it any real thought on your own. You go to a place of worship to fit in - be a part of the club - look respectable, rather than because its where you find spiritual healing and care for your soul. You spend a lot of time in your doctor's office and you know more about the drugs that could be prescribed for your latest vague "illness" than the doctor knows. You hang out with the in crowd - the players - so you can be cool, rather than doing what your heart and soul want to do. Your appearance, dress, hair, etc. conform to whatever sector of society you want to be identified with, rather than asking yourself what feels right to you.

Who are *you*? What do *you* want? Isn't it time we all became adults of the universe?

Imagine

"No hell below us, above us only sky" *Imagine*, John Lennon, September, 1971

Imagine by John Lennon is probably my favorite song. It invites us to imagine, dream, pretend - how our world can be. Lennon's version of how the world can be wouldn't work for everyone I suppose. It works for me. I was a young woman when this song was released - filled with great hope for a peaceful, sane world. Actually, I'm still filled with great hope for a peaceful, sane world.

"Nothing to kill or die for, and no religion too." Did you ever stop and consider how just plain dumb it is for people in power around the world to believe the only way to resolve differences is to kill each other? And, lots of time they are killing and dying for religion. I find it very difficult to believe any higher power or intelligence or love would give our world gold stars for settling our differences by killing each other. Just doesn't make any sense at all.

I'm placing my bet on each of us. We *are* love and sane and shifting to a new place inside. Now, that's something to get excited about. "Imagine all the people living life in peace." Just for a minute consider how many of us on the planet are "living life in peace." Most of us. Not all - I get that - Most!

I also believe in the power of our imagination. It's been said imagination is the voice of god, source, the creator, the universe - pick your favorite word. So, how about we all simply begin spending some time each day in our imagination - imagining the world we want to live in. I wonder if it's just that simple? Somehow, I think it is. John Lennon had the right idea.

"And the world will live as one"

Parallel Realities

Did you ever stop to consider we are all living in parallel realities all the time. This isn't science fiction or a new scientific theory. It's the way life is.

We each create our own reality from our personal experiences and from the choices we make as we journey through life. My sister and I were raised in the same household. Our stories about those years are totally different. We existed in different realities. How many times have you experienced something with a friend. You talk about it afterward and it's as though you had two very different experiences. I've learned from my study of astrology just how differently we each view the world. The lens through which we see the world has many colors and shapes.

So, just for a minute, let's assume we are living in parallel realities. Is it any wonder then that relationships are such a trip? Or, working in a team or for an employer? Or, learning something new? Or, world peace?

I'm writing this sitting here in my reality. This is making perfect sense to me. You are sitting there reading this in your reality. You may be wondering if I've totally lost it. Or, if our realities are similar, you may think I'm not completely wacko.

Learning to let go of our belief that there is only one way - one reality - makes room - helps us expand - so we can truly listen to the other. We don't have to become the other in order to listen with love.

Historically, most religions have been the enemy of peace on earth. Many of them have a fundamental *my way or the highway* teaching - they purposefully create division. To them the concept of parallel realities is foreign. I'm still truly amazed that some have existed for so very long. Maybe the reason is many people are so starved for love they just want to be a part of something? Or, maybe it's the fear of death - or what may come after death? It's very sad that powerful men over time have exploited these human fears.

Back to parallel realities. Peace - inside and out here on this Earth - can come about. It's possible. The thing is - we have to make room for each other and our different realities. There is no right way or wrong way. There are only different ways.

A Theory of Life

Notice I didn't say *the* theory of life - just *a* theory - mine for today. All theories need a formula. Here's mine:

Seeing - Accepting - Choosing - Learning = Wisdom and Joy

I've learned a lot from studying astrology. It helps me see more clearly - myself and others. It's not the only way to clear seeing - it is simply a way. It also has helped me to accept at a deeper level. Accept myself, you, the human journey - this lifetime and all lifetimes. I suppose that's why it has stood the test of time? I know many - most? - people think its new age nonsense. It is a profound, symbolic teaching. And, clearly not for everyone.

So, by whatever means, seeing clearly is the first step. I would add - seeing clearly with/as love. One of the pitfalls of clear seeing is judgment and criticism. Here you are going along in a programmed state - something happens in your life and you get a clear view for a nano second. Now, you think you're some sort of enlightened being. Wrong.

But, you don't know that at the time. From your new, clear seeing, enlightened state you now can see everything that's wrong with me, you and the whole universe. You just fell into the first hole in the road on the way to wisdom. Might take a while - eventually you'll see - really see. You'll know when you are there - it's a very humbling experience and leads to a certainty that you don't know a thing - and, that you are clearly not enlightened. Just a pilgrim on the path. This is the voice of experience talking here!

Now that I clearly see - next comes acceptance. Accepting myself as I am - and you as you are - and, the world as it is. We are unique beings and the same being - all at once. Acceptance doesn't mean passivity. Acceptance does have a lot to do with peace inside - and, out here in the world.

Ok, I see clearly and I accept the world as it is. Now what? Well, now I'm standing on solid ground. Free will exercised from this ground is powerful. From this place Choice is a force in my life. If I choose before I can see clearly and before I can accept life as it is, then my choices may not lead to my desires - I may not even know what my desires are. Here I see, accept what I can change and what I can't change, know my deepest desires, find my courage and Choose. Spirit/Universe/Creator/God/Your Own Word gets a clear message - here we go!

So, I tried something new - a new course in life - a new belief - a new person or place. Did it work out or not? Even if it didn't bring us what we had hoped for, so long as we see life as an opportunity to learn - one long, happy, adventurous road - it really doesn't matter whether it turned out as we envisioned up front. What matters is we had the experience and we learned.

Conscious experience brings us wisdom and joy. When I think about my life - it brings a smile to my face. What a ride! At the time of some of my more intense experiences,

I may not have been able to say that. From this vantage point, I'm grateful for the whole bizarre, sometimes chaotic, ride. Think back over your own life. Where were the lessons and did they ultimately lead to wisdom and joy? If not, I wonder why?

Life is dynamic. Here I stand a wiser soul in some way. The beginning of a new cycle - as a different being - a different view. New things to see clearly, accept, choose and learn. And, so it goes - on and on through our lives - through many lives, if you believe in reincarnation.

I was explaining my theory to a woman one day and she didn't like it all. I think it touched anger - or fear - in her. She wants to believe she can get *there* in this lifetime, rest and not have to do any more *work* - ever. Well, who knows, maybe that will work for her?

Is your life the great adventure - new things to see - new wisdom and joy to experience - cycle after cycle after cycle never ending discoveries?

Psychology or Common Sense?

I enjoy studying psychology, especially the works of C. G. Jung. I began my study in an attempt to see myself more clearly - why do I think and act the way I do?

Psychology and common sense sort of overlap. My Daddy was one wise man - filled to the top with just plain old common sense.

In this section you will find both Jung and Daddy and a few other people who have had a lot to say about who we are and how we might best walk our path.

A few more pieces for your own puzzle.

The Two Most Important Days

"The two most important days in your life are the day you are born and the day you find out why." - Mark Twain

I recently saw this Mark Twain quote and really liked it. Asking why we are born is one of the perennial questions we beings have been contemplating for a very long time.

I wonder why we - all of us - are even here? There was a series on TV a while back - *Life After People*. It aired on the History Channel as a special documentary - had an audience of 5.4 million viewers - the most watched program ever on the History Channel. Its tagline was "Welcome to Earth . . . Population 0." So, 5.4 million people must have had a similar question?

I also wonder why I am here? To me the best way to answer that question is to discover what I really want inside - my desires. Astrology has taught me we each come into this reality as very different beings. Different desires, talents, gifts, challenges, lessons. It's when I can walk my path joyously doing what energizes me that I discover - and, live - why I am here. Life can be a whole lot easier than we make it.

If I attempt to go along with the tribe, then I don't check in with myself. What do I want? If what I want is consistent with the tribe - great. Oftentimes that isn't the case. We are all unique, beautiful beings. The tribe is like committee think - it doesn't represent any one human being - in that way it isn't human. Or, sometimes the tribe has such a powerful leader - it is one person's path that everyone is attempting to follow. Bad plan.

The tribe can be a society, political or religious philosophy, family of origin norms - you can add your own list.

So, why am I here? Why are you here? Pondering these questions could actually help bring about peace on earth.

The Straight Stuff

My Daddy was one of the wisest people I've ever known. He didn't finish high school, so not educated - wise. He also lived his life his own way - an Aquarius sun. Some - many - of his choices were certainly vulnerable to criticism. So, his wisdom was grounded in experience.

I was recently working with a young man who said, "just tell me like it is - what do you see?" I remember asking Daddy for the *answer* many times in my frustration or pain. He would say I'm going to tell you *the straight stuff.*

Here's Daddy's version of the straight stuff. Go back and look at what happened. Where did you act in a way you knew somewhere inside was wrong? What did you do to bring this on yourself? If you don't like the way they are treating you, leave. If you don't like anybody, then be alone. If you don't agree with others, walk away. Just let them be. And on a more global plane - never trust preachers or politicians. Book leaning is OK but it won't help you with life.

That's a sampling. Someday I'm going to write a book about Daddy's take on the world.

So, the straight stuff. We often times want somebody else to give us the answer, especially when we are in the midst of one of life's many storms. The problem is someone else's answer really doesn't have anything to do with you - it is simply the way they see the problem from their vantage point. Their answer might actually sidetrack or derail you.

You also can't find your answer in a doctor's office or from your local drug dealer. TV is an anesthetic, as is sex, exercise, shopping, you fill in the rest. No answers there, either.

Now what? Go inside to your heart or the still small voice or however you conceive of your own innate wisdom - your inner guide. And, listen.

The next step is where the magic happens. Find your courage to act in the way you know in your heart of hearts is right for you.

That's the straight stuff.

What Do You Want?

What do you want? Make a list. Keep adding to it over time. You might even consider prioritizing the list. Now add a statement about why you want that particular item on your list. Next, take one item on your list and think about a small step you could take to get you closer to your want. Then, consider what steps two, three, etc. might be. Before you know it - magic - you have what you want.

Some version of the above process has been taught by just about everybody in the fields of consulting, coaching, mentoring. Simple. Easy. Effective.

So, then why is it we aren't all walking around with everything we want?

My theory.

Most of the time we don't answer the basic question honestly. What do you want? Truly. Really. In your heart of hearts.

And, do you want it enough to *consider* what practical steps will be necessary for you to attain the goal? I'm not even talking about taking the steps or doing the work yet. I'm talking about thinking about and maybe writing the steps necessary. I've found - at about this place in the process - most people go back to just wishing they could have something, rather than setting about to get it.

Consider the Hero's or Heroine's Journey. The first step is you have to leave home. If you don't leave home, you can't go anywhere - at least not out here in this material world.

So, if I want something I don't have, the first step is I have to *leave home* and do something different from my usual way of thinking, believing, talking and acting. Do I want it badly enough to leave home? That's the real question.

Are You on the Stage or in the Audience?

Several years ago I kept having the same dream over and over. I was always on the stage - acting in a play - always some kind of drama. In the next scene of my dream I was *also* in the audience watching the play. Took me a while to understand that dream, but I finally got the lesson and it really changed my life. Here's is how my dream may be able to help you:

Did you ever get caught up in something and wonder how you got so worked up over the whole thing? It could be an argument with your partner. Maybe it's something habitual like your way of relating to your child or co-worker or boss. They just get to you in a way you really don't like.

In these situations - and, many more you can imagine from your own life - you may want to be able to disengage upfront, rather than after much angst.

Consider the metaphor of life as a stage and we are all actors playing our part. The argument begins - you know your lines and you play them well. The other is equally skilled and you both put on quite the show.

Ever notice when your friends are arguing, or all fired up, or stressed - you are sort of naturally disengaged? You listen, but there isn't any emotional charge. The reason is - you are in their audience, watching their play.

So, the next time you find yourself on the stage, getting stressed or angry - consider sitting in the audience and watching the show! Become the observer - the witness. Try it. It's like watching yourself in a movie. You are on the stage speaking your lines *and* you are in the audience watching.

Over time you begin to identify more with the "you" who is in the audience watching the show. And, sort of magically, the "you" on the stage becomes more conscious, too - more at choice. It's a great way to stay grounded and at peace inside.

Boldly Go Where No One Has Gone Before

"The creative is the place where no one else has ever been. You have to leave the city of your comfort and go into the wilderness of your intuition. What you'll discover will be wonderful. What you'll discover will be yourself." - Alan Alda

Did you ever stop to consider you boldly go where no one has gone before every time you access your intuition - a new idea - an inspiration - a creation. Artists boldly go there a lot - some live there. Students, parents, working people, children - creativity makes our lives much, much easier no matter what path we are currently walking.

My logical mind is really good at thinking - finding all the pieces, fitting them together and presenting me with a possible choice or a solution to a problem. Several years ago it occurred to me I didn't have to think my way through life. While my logical mind does a pretty good job, I discovered my intuition was sort of magically right on - a lot. When we are accessing intuition - we are it - no process - no time lapse - we just sort of know whatever we are seeking. Sometimes we aren't even looking for anything. It's just there. Groovy!

Alan Alda says you have to "leave the city of your comfort and go into the wilderness of your intuition." The city of our comfort is thinking. Intuition is more like feeling or being or knowing. Everything is right there - beyond thought - outside of the city of our comfort.

Many of us think to be creative means to be an artist. Not true. We are all *creativity*. It's a state of being. Like love is a state of being. I am love - I am creative - you, too.

Next time you are thinking through an issue or a problem - find your answer by that method. Set it aside and then imagine, dream, feel, intuit - boldly go where no one has gone before - way out there - in the One Mind - space - the universe - pure consciousness - or whatever word you like. "What you'll discover will be wonderful. What you'll discover will be yourself."

Game On

We humans love to play games - everything from football to chess. We play card games, board games, video games, psychological games, social games, religious games, occult games, news media games - add your favorite.

Nothing wrong with games. We discover our creativity - learn strategy - gain knowledge and maybe even become wiser souls. My mind loves to play games.

Years ago there was a phrase that stuck in my head. *Game on!* This has to do with psychological games we all play. The argument begins - he said the one thing he knows pushes my major buttons. Do I let it go or not? Naw - not today. So, I say the one thing that I know pushes all of his buttons. Game on! Nobody wins and we both know that going in. Winning the game is an impossibility. I wonder why we play?

There is a recent movie with a tag line - "play or be played." Is that why? We believe if we don't play - we get played - taken advantage of or end up doing even more stuff we really don't want to do?

I guess we each have our own way in life. No right or wrong. If you enjoy the game - great. If the other enjoys the game - great. Simply realizing you are playing a game can shift the whole thing. What are your rules? How will you know who wins? Will you be friends afterwards - go have a drink or a cup of coffee and talk about how you each played your part?

Discovering Wisdom
When We Realize We Are Love - Everything Shifts

It always amazes me how football players - or, at least, most of them - can play hard against the other team on the field and then walk off as friends. The opponents may even be on the same team next year. Wild.

Is that the way you are playing the game? Good sports?

Relationships

Here's my take on relationships. First and foremost, your relationship with another person can never be any better than your relationship with you. Do you know what you truly want? Are you honest with yourself? Are you pretending your way through life or do you have the courage to see your life and yourself as it and you really are? Do you love yourself exactly as you are?

When we fall in love, the psychologists tell us, we fall in love with the un-owned, but real, parts of ourselves that we project onto the other. We are looking to complete ourselves - with what we already have but don't know it!

So, when you meet a new person, you project onto her all of your un-owned parts. Now she may or may not actually have all those things as part of her makeup. The way our ego works, it really doesn't matter. The ego pretends she does. So, then after some time passes, you say to yourself or her - "you are not the person I met and fell in love with." The truth is she never was. You made her up.

In order to have a mature, lasting relationship with anyone, you have to be able to honestly and truly say to yourself, "no one can give me what I most deeply want or need - only I can do that." However, "I can celebrate and invest in the relationship for what it does give me - companionship, mutual respect, support and the dance of opposites." Since the other person is the opposite of you in some way, no matter who the other person is, it's important that it be a dance - sometimes I get to lead and sometimes you get to lead.

Another way to look at it is - what have your dreams been for yourself and what fears have blocked you. It's back to - who am I and what do I want? What are my true needs - with those two questions and answers as a back-drop. Those basic "this is who I am" kind of needs pretty much can't be negotiated away - at least not for long.

Once you fully realize the other person is not capable of giving you what you want, then you begin the work of realizing only you can do that for you. And, you begin to honor your true needs. And, you find true courage to ask your needs be met.

So, your needs being met vs. empathy for the other. First and foremost your needs - the basic, true, heart needs must be met. You must feel you are respected, validated, feel that you count. I'm not talking about your need to go to a football game here, but your need to be heard and respected. The football game may be an outward sign that you don't feel you are heard.

Empathy means you understand where the other person is coming from. That is a good quality. However, if you aren't feeling honored, all the empathy in the world won't improve the communication between two people.

So, I would say it's more priority. I must feel my true needs are being met - priority one. Then, once I'm standing on solid ground, I can look at the other with empathy for what they are enduring. Anything else is pretending. Trying. Not real. And, what they might be enduring is the consequence of one of my decisions that they don't agree with. "I understand and empathize with you that you don't agree with my decision - this is who I am and what I must do."

So, whose needs get to be met? Both people have that right. Where relationships get really meaningful from a teaching/learning perspective is right here. It goes like this: "I don't want to do A. Well, I do want to do A. OK, I will do B and you do A and I'll see ya tomorrow." It's imperative that each person have the freedom to do, say, think, act as they truly want and that each person is honored for that.

You are not the same. No two people are the same. It is an unrealistic expectation to believe that any two people always want to do the same thing at the same time. When I hear people say that, I know one person is giving themselves away and the other person is happily taking what is being given.

Relationships are filled with compromises. Stephen Covey years ago taught that a relationship is like a bank account. You make deposits and you make withdrawals. If the withdrawals exceed the deposits over time, the relationship is critically out of balance. When this happens sometimes people separate. It's interesting, most often they stay together and "suffer through".

Many of us are trapped in the illusion of being a victim. So, if I am convinced I'm a victim - "Ole poor me!" then I sort of expect you to treat me bad. I expect that bank account to be out of balance. I get to happily skip along being a total victim, usually angry at the world. It's who I am - the tough guy or gal.

There is just one big problem with the person in this relationship who is the "Ole poor me" victim. They spread lots of angst in the world, harm other people and they don't live very long! Being a habitual victim, especially in your close relationships, is the single biggest cause of illness, physical and emotional, on the planet. So, this is really not light weight stuff here.

So, how about the other person in this relationship. Their bank account is also out of balance - the other way. They aren't the victim - they are the child who never grows up. They want and want and want. They take and take and take. And, ironically, they don't feel satisfied. Their issue is that they haven't matured. We have all known spoiled children who get everything and are not grateful for anything. These folks are a lot like that. Health can be an issue for these people since they tend toward addiction - pleasure, drugs, alcohol, food, shopping, you name it.

They will probably outlive the victim and are sort of always unhappy.

I have obviously painted a picture of two extremes. Most of us fall somewhere in this model.

Bottom line - relationships require great courage and are fertile fields for learning about ourselves. They are part of the noble path. If you are serious about the inner journey, you will start with the person lying beside you who is telling you something you don't want to hear about yourself! Listen - they are often times your clearest mirror.

I Don't *Need* You! - Is That Cool or What?

I suppose the technical, psychological term is co-dependency. I guess it's no surprise that so many people are co-dependent with their partner, parents, children, bosses, friends - just about anybody is a great candidate. The reason it's no surprise is we so often don't know the answers to the most basic questions: Who am I? What do I want - right here, right now?

If I don't know who I am or what I want, then I feel I *need* somebody to complete me, or to tell me what to think, or what to do, or to take care of me. This is a really, really big deal. The only life I can live is my own. The only life you can live is your own.

If I want you to live my life - take care of me - tell me what to do, I will be stressed, probably be plagued with illness, unhappy, angry - it just doesn't work. Mostly because you can't do it right.

Responsibility. If I stand up and say what I want and say who I am, then I am responsible for my life. Not you.

I have a good friend who told me years ago that she never wanted to grow up. What she couldn't see then is the only freedom in this whole material lifetime is in growing up and being responsible for what you want - for your choices. Anything short of that and you are living someone else life - trapped in your own immaturity. The completely insane thing is - the only way I can ever feel peace inside, joy, happiness is when I'm doing what I want, being who I am.

So, try out these basic questions: Who are you? What do you want - right here, right now? Who in your life do you *need*? Just how cool are you?

Barriers

"Your task is not to seek for love, but merely to seek and find all the barriers within yourself that you have built against it." - Rumi

Why would we build barriers against love? Lots of reasons. I love you and you hurt me in some way - I build a barrier to protect me from you. Barrier building usually begins when we are very young - children, teens, young adults. It's almost as if life is set up so that we must build barriers to protect ourselves. Oftentimes, the wounds go deep and the barriers are high and thick. True love may allude us our entire lives.

One of the problems with barriers is they tend to wall off all love. Before we know it we can't feel love from any source - divine or human. We begin living in a barren place - in the middle of a field of pure love we can't feel.

It takes great courage to "find all the barriers within yourself" and allow them to dissolve.

Why not consider giving yourself the gift of love? Look inside. Where have you built walls - either to protect yourself and/or to keep others out? Why not take a leap and let them fall away? Remember Ebenezer Scrooge in *A Christmas Carol*? It was written in 1843. We've been building barriers for a very long time.

Hate Is Too Great a Burden to Bear

"I have decided to stick with love. Hate is too great a burden to bear." - Martin Luther King, Jr.

I've always admired Martin Luther King, Jr. He was a clergyman, activist and leader in the civil rights movement in the US. He received the Nobel Peace Prize in 1964 for combating inequality through nonviolence. He was assassinated on April 4, 1968 - a true tragedy.

"Hate is too great a burden to bear." Have you ever found yourself angry with someone? So angry you are over the top - you might even say you hate them? We all have. Think about how you feel inside when you are in an angry place. Muscles are tight, you are stressed, a scowl on your face, gritting your teeth, and lots of other physical indications that all is not well inside. Many people live in this place a lot. No wonder even medical science now acknowledges stress as a precursor to many diseases. I would add - most. Our bodies feel the *burden* when we choose angry thoughts - when we choose hate.

"I've decided to stick with love." I wonder if it's just that simple? A decision - a choice. Not to hate. Just think about that a minute. We are all free to choose. Let's all simply choose to *stick with love*. Peace on earth - over night - now that's magic.

I See You

I liked the film *Avatar* - during its run it broke all box office records and became the highest grossing film of all time and was the first film to gross more than $2 billion.

The Na'Vi - the people native to Pandora in the film - greet each other by saying "I see you." As they explain, "I see you" doesn't mean ordinary seeing - it means "I see myself in your eyes." Similar to the Buddhist greeting Namaste - the god in me sees the god in you.

That phrase "I see you" has really stayed with me. How often do we talk to one another, work together, live together, go to school together, think we are friends, lovers, parents and never really *see* each other?

Do you feel, at times, few people actually *see* you? Sometimes I think I must be invisible. I really like spending time with people who look in my eyes and are *there* when we are talking. Aren't those energizing times? A real soul connection.

Likewise, I am very capable of going through the motions in conversations and not really being there or really seeing the other. So, in my life anyway, it works both ways.

Use the Na'Vi meaning of "I see myself in your eyes." How often are you truly *with* the person sitting next to you?

No Matter Where You Go - There You Are!

The above quote is attributed to Confucius (551 BC - 479 BC)

What great wisdom! This is another way to say that who and what I encounter in the world is a reflection of me.

If you're complaining about clerks in a store who are not courteous - there you are. If your best friend is a martyr or a victim or too emotional - there you are. Conversely, if you see tenderness and love in the eyes of a friend - there you are. If you find yourself with some very creative, upbeat people - there you are. You get the idea.

A popular phrase these days is "like attracts like." That means people with similar qualities tend to like each other. So, if you have a friend or a partner - you feel a certain mutual attraction - great. Then the day comes when you find yourself criticizing this person. Just know, most likely, you share the same attribute you are criticizing in the other - like attracts like. Sometimes a bitter pill to swallow.

It seems to me the greatest gift we can give ourselves and the world is to know ourselves better - learn to look honestly in the mirror of self awareness. Unfortunately, we can't leave ourselves at home when we go out in the world, so we will attract people and situations to us that are a reflection of us. If you want to know your lessons in this life, just look around - they are looking back at you.

No matter where *you* go - there *you* are!

What if You Just Decide to be Happy?

We each get to choose the thoughts we think. That sounds like an obvious statement. Where that statement gets complicated is in living it. If it's true we are the chooser, then why is it we choose to be other than at peace, happy and joyful all the time? Here's my theory.

My intention is to live my life in a place of inner peace. I'm serious about this intention. I decided to live in this way several years ago. It's amazing how much my life has changed so that I can be in alignment with that intention. I became very aware of what disturbed my peace. I discovered for the most part it was my own thoughts.

In my every day world, friends and loved ones would say or do something that triggered emotion in me. I would get hurt, or afraid, or angry, or sad, or feel sorry for myself. In my heightened state of observer I watched the triggering event (someone out there in the world) and then I would watch my emotional reaction. I realized I have no control over the triggering events in my life - *and*, I have total and complete control over my emotional reaction.

So, the only trick was to figure out how to change my thoughts when I encountered a triggering event. It occurred to me I needed a guiding principle - some thought to replace the fearful, angry, etc. thoughts. I decided to just be at peace and happy. Now, when I sense thoughts that are taking me down a road I don't want to go, I stop. I realize the negative thought is not consistent with my intention and replace it with a new thought - "I am at peace and happy."

I'm not talking about repressing emotions or not being authentic - I'm all for authenticity and honestly feeling emotions. I'm simply pointing out that you have a choice about what you think.

Next, I looked around at who and what in my life were the major triggers. Now, I rarely place myself in a position where I'm with those people or in those situations. I *cleaned up* my life. Sort of like cleaning out a closet. I still have a few old things back there in the back of the closet - they will go eventually.

I wonder how your life would change if you just decided to be happy?

Here I Stand A Stronger Soul

"Hurrah! I did the thing I feared the most. Excuse me while I cheer. Now here I stand a stronger soul and all I've lost is fear." - Anonymous

Several years ago a wise person gave me the above quote and I've looked at it every day since. Lots of wisdom in this one simple statement.

"I did the thing I feared the most." Before I can *do* the thing I fear the most, I have to *see* the thing I fear the most. So, how can I see the thing I fear the most? Here are some clues.

You may find yourself saying something like this: "Oh, it really doesn't matter, anyway." "I really didn't want to do/have/say that." "It's not important."

Or, you may find yourself sort of *habitually* angry over an issue or at a certain person. Just know that habitual anger *always* sits on top of fear.

OK, let's say you have discovered a fear you hold. Now, you are at a choice point. Are you going to do the thing you fear the most? And doing it looks like this:

You say what is true for you even though you know the other person may not like what you have to say and you are fearful of their reaction.

Even though an action you may want to take seems fearful, you find your courage and take the action in the face of your fears - leaving a relationship or a job.

When you are angry, you have the courage to see your fear that is fueling the anger.

Consider doing the thing you fear the most. And, remember, all you'll lose is fear.

Peace

A lot of us talk about wanting a world filled with peace. Did you ever stop to seriously think about how *you* would have to change in order for all of us to live on this beautiful blue planet together in peace?

I wonder if peace is possible. I wonder if the people of earth have ever lived in peace.

We each, at our core, belong to a clan - at least in our early years - some for a lifetime. Identifying with the clan gives us *a very limited identity*. You can also think of the clan as a system or systems of thought.

This leads us to *ideologies* - defined as: 1. The body of *ideas* reflecting the social needs and aspirations of an individual, group, class, or culture. 2. A set of doctrines or *beliefs* that form the basis of a political, philosophical, economic, religious, scientific or other system.

In our world here in the US these ideologies are constantly reinforced in the media, advertising, education - you fill in the rest. So, our minds are conditioned to be a part of the clan.

The Hatfields and McCoys refers to a feud between two families (1863 - 1891). The story of this feud has become a modern symbol of the *perils* of family honor, justice, and vengeance.

All conflict arises from ideological *differences*.

So, look around your own life. Where do you have differences with other people, belief systems, cultures - to the extent you find yourself in an angry, non-peaceful place when thinking of them or dealing with them?

Peace can only be created by peaceful people.

If you and I honor each other, we can disagree in a peaceful way. No *One Truth* - only *truths*. We each have our own path to walk - our own lessons to learn - our own view of the world given our state of awareness.

I've been reading a lot about science recently and scientific theories. Lots of very smart, good people attempting to solve the great mysteries of life. They seem a lot like the Hatfields and McCoys - different clans - feuding. What a waste of energy.

I read on the NASA site only 5% of the universe is known matter - and some of that is still a mystery. I wonder how small that number - 5% - will become once our ability to see further and further into the cosmos improves. My guess is the universe is vast and *diverse* beyond what our conscious minds can comprehend. We are attempting to arrive at a theory of everything with only an infinitesimal sample of the universe at our disposal.

I use this as an example of how feuds begin and are perpetuated. The problem for scientists working in this area is they have almost no facts - once you consider the vastness of the unknown. So the feud over *theories* continues. I wonder why?

What does this have to do with peace? Remember - peace can only be created by peaceful people. To the extent any one of us finds ourselves feuding with an opposing clan we are *not* contributing to peace. Scientists are really, really smart, well educated people and even they haven't found a way to live peace within their discipline.

Where in your life are you feuding with another clan?

Conflict is a part of being human - at least in these times. Solving conflict in a peaceful way is a skill that can be learned. It is based on speaking with respect, honoring our differences and not trying to convert the other person to our way of thinking. There is no one right idea. There are as many right ideas as there are human beings.

I wonder how our lives would be different if we shifted the energy presently being spent in conflict and rechanneled it into creativity? Imagination, intuition - the language of the soul - our deeper being. In that place we *are* peace - and love.

Anger - The Doorway to Fear

Isn't it amazing that we can be in the best place emotionally - happy, enjoying life - and, here comes a wave crashing down on our heads. Someone out there in the world says or does something. It's kind of like they open a door and here comes the raging tiger - anger.

When that happens to me, one part of me feels and expresses the anger while another part of me sort of watches the show. Sounds right down schizophrenic! Actually it's not. And, there is always a lesson where there is anger. I am aware enough to know that my anger really has absolutely nothing to do with the person who opened the door. It has to do with what I see on the other side of the door.

Rather than repress emotions, acknowledging them and looking for the lesson is a healthier way to react. In my case the door often times opens on my fear of being controlled - of not being able to live my own life.

Anger always sits on top of fear. So, any time you are angry or if you are around others who are angry - just know there is great fear under all that anger. The angrier a person is the more fear buried deep inside.

Once I can see the fear underneath the anger, I am on my way to learning the lesson the emotion of anger brings to me. The goal is to deal with the fear that sort of lies in the shadow beyond the door.

Viewed from the standpoint of myth, the dragon you are to slay on your hero's journey is most often fear. Some are hidden deep in caves. Some under the water. Usually they require an adventure to find and slay.

What is the fear behind your anger - the dragon you are to slay?

Costumes

"In most of our human relationships, we spend much of our time reassuring one another that our costumes of identity are on straight." - Ram Dass

So, in relationship we mutually assure each other that the costumes we are wearing look great. Sort of like - hey - that is a great outfit or pair of shoes. You look really cool! Nice hair. Love the color of your nail polish. Hey, Man, neat watch. You get the picture. These examples are one kind of costume we wear.

I believe Ram Dass is describing a completely different kind of costume. He is talking about "costumes of identity." We all construct our world - every small and large part of it. First, *we construct ourselves*. We choose a costume. In astrology your costume is somewhat associated with your rising sign - sometimes defined as the mask you wear for the world. It's not who you really are inside. It's the optimal mask you have chosen to wear - your costume.

Nothing wrong with wearing a mask for the world or even in a relationship. Nothing wrong with assuring each other that our "costumes of identity are on straight."

The hole in the road here is when you confuse who you really are inside with the mask - the costume. And, when those close to you overly identity with the "you" who is the mask, rather than the real you. Think of it as an actor or actress on the stage. You play a great role. However, when the show is over, it's time to take off the costume and become the real authentic you.

Relationship is between two real people - not two masks - not two costumes.

Stop a minute and think about whether you are always "on" or whether you have people, places, moments in your life where you can take off the mask and be the beautiful, unique, authentic you.

Zombies and Vampires

The land of the walking dead - will-less, speechless walking dead capable of automatic movement who have died and been supernaturally reanimated. Or, the reanimated body of a dead person who comes from the grave at night and sucks the blood of living people. Wow. And, these walking dead are very, very popular right now - we are calling this entertainment.

Psychology would teach us that the horror we appreciate most tends to mirror what's going on in our lives.

So, where are *we* the walking dead - will-less - speechless - moving automatically through life? Where have we died inside? Who's life blood are we sucking - or, who is sucking our life blood?

Here are a couple possibilities:

We've been experiencing one of the longest, possibly worst, economic recession in a long time. Do we all feel the life blood is being sucked out of us? Viewed from a spiritual perspective, the recession is a good thing. It has the potential to help us escape from materialism. What's important? Really? A bigger house, newer car, latest fashion, you fill in the rest - or peace inside? And, it's hard to see the spiritual side when the economic reality is staring you in the face.

Where are we the walking dead, will-less, speechless, moving automatically through life? Who am I? What do I want? We each have free will - we are the choosers in our life. Isn't that just the greatest thing ever? Step out of the known into the unknown - the field of all possibilities. In that field there are no walking dead.

On a personal level vampires may reflect a deep anxiety over receiving insufficient nurturance - we may feel sucked dry inside - that others are feeding on us. One of the Vampire series on TV turned this act into something sexy and desirable. Sounds a lot like co-dependence?

The world is changing and time is passing at warp speed.

A popular way these days to reach out to each other is to post on Facebook, Twitter or to send a text message. Most cell phones are kept on forward. It may be rare to even have the human being you are calling actually answer the phone. So, voice mail talks to voice mail. Virtual reality games are very popular.

I love technology and think it's great that people are virtually touching each other - a good thing. This book allows me to virtually touch you.

I also think it's important we remember virtual relationship isn't the same as real relationship. We are living beings and we thrive when we are in the presence of other living beings we love and who love us. It's important we are *seen* by real, physical, in our presence eyes. Remember *Avatar* - I see you - I see myself in your eyes - a soul connection.

I guess we'll just have to see how long it takes the Zombies and Vampires to go back to the grave and stay there. Remember, there are no walking dead in the field of all possibilities.

Looking For Love In All The Wrong Places

There is an old Waylon Jennings' country song by this name. To me the song is great, and the name of the song speaks volumes. How can we look for love in all the wrong places?

How many people do you know who look for love in a doctor's office or in a prescription bottle? They probably got the message when they were a small child that you get a lot of attention and love when you're sick. How about the person who looks for love as the rebel? Or, the perpetual child? Or, the warrior - can't you just see him or her standing in the middle of the floor, stomping their foot as a three year old? They got attention, which to a child equals love.

Some people are over achievers, Type A personalities, always trying. That was me for many years. I got the message when I was young that I had to *try* to be good enough, to get attention or love. I was rewarded with praise when I did something adult-like. Otherwise, I was sort of just there. So, I worked and worked and worked and tried and tried and tried. I finally saw my pattern a few years back. No more trying for me - or, at least, that's my intention - old programs die hard.

The thing is we don't have to look for love at all. We are love! Deepak Chopra and Ram Dass have both said we are all god in drag. God, the divine, source, the universe, the field - in drag - dressed as one role - human in this material world - while actually being another - spirit.

Can you see you *are* love? Or, are you still looking for love in all the wrong places?

Some words from Ram Dass to help us on our way: "As you dissolve into love, your ego fades. You're not thinking about loving; you're just being love, radiating like the sun."

The Genesis of Pain

We all experience emotional pain from time to time. Did you ever stop and wonder where the pain comes from? It goes like this. Something happens out there in the world. Maybe a person I love acts in a way that is hurtful to me. I feel pain.

Now, if I hang onto that pain, I suffer. The Buddhists teach pain is a part of life and suffering is optional - or, words to that effect.

Back to pain. Emotional pain is born when I don't want to accept the reality of my life. OK, someone hurt me. If I can accept the action of the other as a part of my reality, the pain doesn't grow. I feel it. It's fleeting and tends to dissipate quickly. When pain hangs around for awhile, it is most likely because I'm attempting to pretend that the reality of my life is something else. Or, I wish it could be another way. Or, I'm in total denial about what happened in the first place. Sort of attempting to fool myself it isn't so bad after all.

When we can turn around and look life in the eye and accept what is, then pain is diminished or simply evaporates.

Now to suffering. Suffering is simply hanging onto pain. It's a choice. Again, here I'm talking about emotional pain. We keep reliving the original perceived wrong - over and over. We get stuck in that place of why me? Or, how could that person have done that? Rather than simply accepting life as it is - whatever happened, happened - and, realizing suffering is a choice.

Learning to let go is a very useful practice. See it, feel it, accept the reality of it all and let it go. Tomorrow you may be the one causing another being pain. We are all in this little dance called life together. And, it ain't always goodness, light and holding hands as we dance into the sunset.

The advanced course teaches that we also *forgive* the other. Whoa! I read someplace forgiveness is for *me* - it sets me free. How cool is that?

The Hidden Meaning of Illness

In *The Hidden Meaning of Illness, Disease as a Symbol and Metaphor* Bob Trowbridge presents a different way to view illness. Following are some highlights from this book that added a few more pieces to the puzzle of life I'm always attempting to put together.

Did you ever consider that illness from colds to cancer is meaningful and that the illness is experienced within a life that is meaningful?

Illness has meaning in the same way that dreams have meaning. Like symbols in our dreams, our illnesses are messages from the psyche - the inner self - which can be interpreted and understood. Our illnesses are not really the problem - they are only a symbol or symptom of the problem. The root problem is always spiritual - an imbalance or distortion in our thinking, attitudes and feelings.

Every ache and pain in the body is a message to the mind. It's a call for help. Something is out of balance.

Holistic medicine sees the individual as a mind-body system, not as a machine with parts. Illness is seen as a problem involving the whole individual, not just one part. All illnesses represent, at some level, a "dis-ease" of the soul, an imbalance of the body and spirit. The mind is the intermediary between the two. It is a given that the mind can make the body sick or well. If the mind makes the body sick, it does so for a reason.

Discovering Wisdom
When We Realize We Are Love - Everything Shifts

Imagine your mind as a pipe. Divine energy is poured into one end of the pipe. Inside the pipe your mind modifies that energy. Pouring out the other end is the results of your thoughts and intentions. The Universe has a positive intent for us. Therefore, it takes a great deal of energy to make ourselves poor, unhappy or sick. Still, we are free to take divine energy and shape it as we will. Our ability to make ourselves unhappy or sick demonstrates how powerful we are.

A serious illness may be the result of many months or years of your thoughts. When you deny the power of your own thoughts, you confirm yourself as helpless.

An illness has been created in the body to give us information about the deeper, spiritual imbalance. The illness gives us an opportunity to make healing changes in our lives. Healing changes take courage - courage to act, to apply our insights and to make difficult healing choices.

Courage is the daughter of love. Fear is the opposite of love and courage. Love and courage are the antidotes of fear.

Illness can give us a chance to get back on a life affirming track. Illness presents challenges - all challenges have doors to a new way of being.

Death by illness. Sometimes illness is a way to leave this life. Living for many years is not a measure of a healthy or fulfilling life. Some people may simply complete their life work at an early age and it's time to leave. The success of a life is not determined by how many years an individual lives, but by the quality of the life lived and how much love the life contained.

Being responsible for your illness is not the same as being blamed for your illness. Responsibility has to do with accountability. It's empowering - you are at choice and can change.

We can change the body by dealing with how we feel. If we ignore our despair, the body receives a "die" message. If we deal with our pain and seek help, then the message is "living is difficult, but desirable," and the immune system works to keep us alive.

This book is mainly directed to people who have chosen the physical body as their major life classroom. Where are you challenged? Where do you handle things well? Think of understanding illness as a detective story, a holy quest or a deep initiation into the mysteries. Be open to finding the hidden reason behind your illness. Look at any illness as a puzzle to be solved. No anger at yourself or at your illness.

The first question is: "Do you want to be healed?" Often illnesses serve us in some way - protecting us from success or failure or the unknown. Or, we receive something from the illness - love, attention.

A serious illness can teach us to live each day more fully. Spiritual growth is an ongoing process with no final destination. It's important to love and appreciate ourselves in all circumstances.

This book is a life journey into the self - a healing journey.

I have given a high level overview of the main theories. Most of the book is very detailed giving ways to assess illnesses and to heal them - all based on the mind-body model and illness as a spiritual journey.

The Privilege of Owning Yourself

"The individual has always had to struggle to keep from being overwhelmed by the tribe. If you try it, you will be lonely often, and sometimes frightened. But no price is too high to pay for the privilege of owning yourself." - Friedrich Nietzsche

Friedrich Wilhelm Nietzsche (1844 - 1900) was a German philologist, philosopher, cultural critic, poet and composer. He wrote several critical texts on religion, morality, contemporary culture, philosophy and science. Central to his philosophy is the idea of "life-affirmation", which involves questioning of any doctrine that drains one's expansive energies, however socially prevalent those ideas might be. He had a very challenging life - many physical and mental problems. "God is dead" is a famous quote. Some thought he was an atheist, some that he was predicting the scientific view, others that he had a clear view of divinity. And, yet, he is thought of by many - not all - to have put forth some important ideas.

My take away from reading some of his works is his emphasis on "owning yourself." He clearly saw how being a member of the tribe can rob each of us of who we are. I'm always amazed how easily we are programmed.

I attended a class in my 40s with others of a similar age. The teacher was helping us see how we had been programmed over the course of our lives. He played jingles from commercials that aired on TV 25 years prior to the class. He would only play one note and then the next and then the next. It was scary how quickly we could identify the jingle, sing the entire thing and remember exactly the visual that went with it back years ago. Totally useless information to be carrying around in our data banks. And, yet, it was there in its entirely. This was one of many exercises to show us the extent to which we had been programmed by marketing and the media. It was frightening. Reminiscent of *1984* by Orwell.

That class taught me a lot. I totally stopped watching TV - I don't want to be programmed. Plus, I discovered a great deal of additional time to pursue what I truly love.

Cigarette commercials were taken off TV after the link between smoking and lung cancer was discovered. Only to be replaced by commercials for drugs. Marketing professionals are trained to create a need so their product can fill it. I wonder when everyone will wake up and these commercials, too, will cease? How many diseases are being created in the very open minds of viewers? How many programs are being installed?

When I put this together with the power of belief that has been shown by many scientific experiments, it makes me wonder about the general health of most people over the coming years? Seems like we are playing with fire?

So, back to Nietzsche - "The individual has always had to struggle to keep from being overwhelmed by the tribe."

And, to me, the struggle is critical. How else will I ever have the privilege of owning myself?

The Doors We Open and Close Each Day Decide the Lives We Live.

The above title is a quote from Flora Whittemore (1890 - 1993)

Flora Whittemore is speaking of doors in our minds. We are the choosers - where do we choose to walk in this minute?

What doors have you never opened - or, opened once and didn't like what you saw on the other side and quickly closed?

Some doors into our inner selves are opened by others in our life. Often they are showing us a brilliant, beautiful, joyous aspect of ourselves we didn't know existed. Really good teachers are great at opening doors. They show us our creative gifts or our interest in a subject we had never considered. Or, an aspect of ourselves we didn't know existed.

Often those with whom we share a close or intimate relationship open doors for us. Sometimes we like what we see and the door remains open. Sometimes we either don't want to accept what is on the other side of the door or it frightens us - that door is probably closed fairly quickly. If we are in a soul centered relationship, the other will keep opening the door until we have the courage to walk through and claim that part of ourselves.

This has to do with seeing clearly - all the parts of us - those we label good and those we label bad. We are each a spark of the divine - Deepak Chopra teaches we are made of stardust. I guess he's right if you accept the big bang theory. All energy and matter came into existence at once - so it follows we are stardust.

The Buddha taught we are born total and complete lacking nothing. All good and all bad are in us. Free will, in a way, is our ultimate test. Of all the infinite possibilities available to me what do I choose to - say, think, become, see, do? So, look at the totality of who you are - all the parts - own them all. And, realize you are the chooser - it's up to you what you manifest in this world.

Back to our doors. What doors have been open for awhile and it might be time to close? Beliefs that have changed. People who were nourishing at one point and are no longer? Have you reached a destination? Is it time for a new journey?

Remember - the doors we open and close each day decide the lives we live.

Enemies

"If you can cultivate the right attitude, your enemies are your best spiritual teachers because their presence provides you with the opportunity to enhance and develop tolerance, patience and understanding." - Dalai Lama XIV

Well, that sort of turns the whole thing around doesn't it? You mean I'm supposed to be grateful for people who irritate me, are greedy, self-centered, mean, childish? You can add your own list.

I don't think the Dalai Lama is saying to excuse them or approve of them. I think what he is saying is to see that their presence in your life has the potential to bring you great teaching.

OK, so let's say you are my enemy. Sort of always in my face, never have anything good to say to me, always doing your own thing and generally don't seem to care about me. If I can see you as my spiritual teacher, rather than a pain in the neck, you present me with the opportunity to walk my spiritual talk. Can I stay centered in who I am, in inner peace? Can I look at you with compassion and understanding? Can I look beyond your words and actions to the human being you are inside? A tall order.

Now, I don't believe this means I stay in your presence, or that I seek you out. It simply means when you are in my life, I don't allow my energy to entrain with yours. I stay centered, know who I am and consciously practice compassion for you.

Isn't it wild. We often become that which we don't like. You are angry, so I become angry in an effort to protect myself. I wonder why you don't become peaceful in an effort to regain your ground of being? I wonder how the world would change if we each held who we are in the face of adversity - strong, steady, centered, at peace inside. Who knows maybe your anger would lessen - maybe if I show compassion, you will soften?

Sorrow Prepares You for Joy

"Sorrow prepares you for joy. It violently sweeps everything out of your house, so that new joy can find space to enter. It shakes the yellow leaves from the bough of your heart, so that fresh, green leaves can grow in their place. It pulls up the rotten roots, so that new roots hidden beneath have room to grow. Whatever sorrow shakes from your heart, far better things will take their place." - Rumi

A friend recently sent me the above Rumi quote. I've been reading Rumi for years and had never come across this quote. It's beautiful and so very true. I have a different friend who has been going through a sorrow filled time - grieving the death of a very close friend. I hope Rumi's very wise and beautiful words help her as she journeys to the other side of grief and ultimately to joy.

"To live many lives, you have to die many deaths" - this sounds like it originated in Eastern thought - not sure where I first heard it. This could be talking about reincarnation. To me it is talking about "dying" to our old selves as we learn and mature. I have died to being a small child, a teenager, to being a young mother of small children, to being a business woman - as my life has unfolded, it has been important for me to be reborn into new aspects or phases of life.

At each "death" I felt great sorrow - grieving what had been and was no more. At times I still yearn to hold my young babies again - both grown adults now. I still hold them - just in a different way - honoring them as adults walking their own path. I know many women who continue to relate to their grown children as if they were babies - they attempt to control them or put them on a guilt trip for not doing as "Mom" says. You see, learning to die is very important.

The cells in our bodies that refuse to die are called cancer.

Remember: "Whatever sorrow shakes from your heart, far better things will take their place."

As you walk along your own hero's or heroine's journey, take time to consciously feel sorrow for what is dying or has died in your life. What's new, what's next? You'll never know until you let go of the "rotten roots, so that new roots hidden beneath have room to grow." Always remembering "sorrow prepares you for joy."

The Only Thing I Have to Fear Is Me

The only thing you have to fear is you. Remember the FDR quote: "The only thing we have to fear is fear itself." This is a little different twist on that idea.

I don't believe there are evil forces at work in the world. There is only us - human beings - screwing up, falling on our face, hurting ourselves and other people, learning, growing.

Karma - what I do is what I get - or words to that effect. I'm walking down a street at night and another human being attacks me and hurts me. Why me, why right now? Like attracts like. Who am I wanting to hurt - maybe emotionally, maybe physically? Or, maybe I feel I've harmed another and deserve some sort of punishment?

I lose my job. I'm downsized - what a lousy word. Why me. Why not the person at the desk beside me. Was I sitting there convinced I was going to be the next one? The universe gives us what we desire. Maybe financially - was I pretty set and not really wanting to be there. People get love from lack - ole poor me - will you feel sorry for me now? Lots of people self sabotage. I could go on with other examples. You get the idea.

Conscious or not, our thoughts create our world.

Now, this is an idea that is not very popular - especially with people who have lots of difficulties in their lives. If you are reading this and thinking this woman is full of it!

Then I ask you - how do you think you will ever get out of the place you seem to be in? Do you think its fate? Your cross to bear this time through? Or, will you consider - just for a moment - if you change, so will the world around you? Andrew Cohen - "Everybody wants to be enlightened but nobody wants to change." How very true. We oftentimes cling to the status quo, even if it brings us pain.

We are a field of limitless possibilities. The universe/spirit/god/creator/whatever word you like - gives us exactly what we ask for. Some people say we are co-creators. This concept has been taught by many - most - traditions over the ages. We create our reality. Simple and magical as that. Life is incredibly easy.

The question then becomes what reality am I creating? In our society many beings want to remain children. They don't believe their life is up to them. Consider taking some time today and thinking about what you are creating in your life. Love or Fear?

The only thing you have to fear is your own conscious/unconscious thoughts and actions.

Wow! Think how powerful you are. Is that awesome or what?

I Can't Believe You

"I'm not upset that you lied to me, I'm upset that from now on I can't believe you." - Friedrich Nietzsche

Sounds harsh doesn't it? After all, each of us has most likely lied about something at some point in our lives. When you were a small child, did you ever lie just to see if you could get away with it? Or, maybe as a teenager or young adult, lying about your age or the time you got home last night or who you were with? Husbands lie to wives and wives lie to husbands. Usually it's about money. Sometimes it's about who you were with or what you were doing - old habits die hard. I could go on and on - you can add your own lies to the list. We usually put these kinds of lies into the white lie category and think nothing of them.

An occasional white lie, I guess, doesn't make so much difference. It's habitual lying that's the problem. And, the real problem is when we lie to ourselves. When I lie to me, I can't even depend on myself - can't even believe myself.

When I lie to me, what does that look like? I say yes to someone when inside my heart of hearts I am screaming no! And, next I tell myself I really do want to do whatever has been asked of me - that's the lie part! How many things are being asked of you - in the name of tradition, family, friends, religious ritual, society - you get the idea - that you don't want to do. And, yet, you march the march. Do the right thing, keep the peace, don't hurt anyone's feelings. You may even tell yourself you want to do these things.

Why would you lie to yourself? Maybe because if you told yourself the truth, then you would have to find your courage and act in a way that's true for you.

You see? Mostly, don't lie to yourself - it's really important that *you* can believe *you*.

Science or Science Fiction?

I've been a science fiction fan for years. It's amazing to me how accurately many science fiction writers have predicted the future. Where do the ideas for science fiction writers come from? Imagination.

Hard core science is based on theories and research. Where do scientific theories come from? Imagination. It seems to me theories may be based on more information - more research - but, they are at least cousins with good science fiction. I expect scientists reading this would beg to differ with me?

Edgar Cayce taught the concept of the One Mind. Jung - the collective unconscious. It seems imagination may be our way of accessing this storehouse of all knowledge and all wisdom? I wonder what would happen if scientists were taught how to imagine - how to intuit - along with classes concerning the physical world and their craft?

I believe we have too many compartments - too many separate disciplines. Too much raw, unorganized information. And, too little imagination, intuition and wisdom. No real way to make sense of or utilize this growing data base. I wonder why we continue to amass it all?

In this section my intention is to provide information from some scientists who it seems to me have gotten out of the box and discovered different ways to view our world. I'm also including book summaries, overviews and excerpts from a few authors who have done a fantastic job of putting together some of this new science.

Science is also running into spirit. I love it! I've also included some of that information.

We live in a magical, mysterious world. Our logical minds keep attempting to trivialize it all. To fit the unseen into the seen.

My sincere hope is for a scientific revolution - one in which old core beliefs are seriously questioned, consciousness is integrated into inquiry and scientists at long last are encouraged to work together.

There is a Field - I'll Meet You There

"Out beyond ideas of wrongdoing and rightdoing there is a field. I'll meet you there. When the soul lies down in that grass the world is too full to talk about." - Rumi

These days quantum physicists talk about the Unified Field or the Zero Point Field as a theory that explains everything. Our universe may be a sea of energy - one vast quantum field. If this is true, everything is connected to everything else - like some invisible web.

Deepak Chopra: "Everything in nature is evolving to a higher level of existence. Even without trying or thinking, just by virtue of our existence itself, we are evolving to a higher level of awareness. When we are aware of this, we evolve even faster. The unified field balances everything in creation–the ecology of nature, the physiology of the human body, the evolution of a human fetus into a baby."

The quote from Rumi at the top of this page is from 800 plus years ago. I've read this quote many, many times. It just occurred to me recently maybe Rumi was talking about the same *field* that is being "discovered" or "theorized" by our best thinkers today.

Miracles

The entire Universe and everything in it is a miracle. You are a miracle. Me, too. Every day, every breath, every heart beat everywhere and everywhen.

Miracle comes from the Latin *miraculum* - a wonder, marvel or to wonder at. Here's a modern definition of miracle: "A surprising and welcome event that is not explicable by natural or scientific laws and is therefore considered to be divine."

". . . not explicable by natural or scientific laws. . ." As I have learned more and more about natural and scientific laws, I realize they are mostly *theories*, not laws - and, that the old theories are not in such good shape these days.

So, the more I realize that not much can be explained by scientific *laws*, I realize most everything is a miracle. At least for today. Maybe tomorrow someone will make a solid scientific discovery that will be able to explain mind, thought, intuition, emotion, intelligence, consciousness, love, joy, gravity, dark matter, dark energy, astrology, psychic abilities, the big bang.

I really didn't know what dark matter and dark energy are. Turns out I'm not alone. This from the NASA site:

"More is unknown than is known. We know how much dark energy there is because we know how it affects the Universe's expansion. Other than that, *it is a complete mystery*. But it is an important mystery. It turns out that roughly 68% of the Universe is dark energy. Dark matter makes up about 27%. The rest - everything on Earth, everything ever observed with all of our instruments, all normal matter - adds up to less than 5% of the Universe. Come to think of it, maybe it shouldn't be called 'normal' matter at all, since it is such a small fraction of the Universe."

So, there you go! Miracles all around - at least 95% of the Universe - not explicable. And, of the 5% that is called normal matter - lots of that isn't explicable, either. Miracles everywhere.

Miracle: "A surprising and welcome event . . . .considered to be divine." We all define the *divine* in our own way. For me its love, as a state of being. To a scientists it may be things unexplainable. To a religious person it may be god.

When you get right down to it, it really doesn't matter how we conceive of the divine - unless we want to fight over the definition and kill each other - what matters is we live in a miracle. So, let's consider living and exploring that miracle, rather than spending so much time trying to fit the mystery into the known.

Does Science Know The Truth?

"Bad religion is arrogant, self-righteous, dogmatic and intolerant. And so is bad science. But unlike religious fundamentalists, scientific fundamentalists do not realize that their opinions are based on faith. They think they know the truth." - Rupert Sheldrake

Dr. Sheldrake is an innovative scientist. In his book, *Science Set Free, 10 Paths to New Discovery*, he questions basic scientific dogmas. When I read his book, I realized even in science we are sort of stuck in the past.

Science today claims all reality is material or physical. Until we can see it, it doesn't exist. But what of consciousness? For the most part, hard core science views the brain as physical matter and somehow consciousness is a byproduct of it. All matter is unconscious. Evolution is purposeless. God/spirit/creator/source/divine is only an idea - a concept - invented by humans to help alleviate our fear of death.

Several basic, materialistic scientific beliefs became dominant in the 19th century and are now taken for granted as the ground upon which all serious research is based. In Dr. Sheldrake's book he states 10 core beliefs and then, in the spirit of scientific inquiry, he asks 10 questions and puts forth a possible answer to each. One such core belief is everything is essentially mechanical, including us. Here is his suggested new way to view this belief:

"The mechanistic theory is based on the metaphor of the machine. But it's only a metaphor. Living organisms provide better metaphors for organized systems at all levels of complexity, including molecules, plants and societies of animals, all of which are organized in a series of inclusive levels, in which the whole at each level is more than the sum of the parts, which are themselves wholes at a lower level. The entire universe is more like a growing, developing organism than a machine slowly running out of steam."

Another core belief is minds are inside heads. Dr. Sheldrake's proposed new way to view the location of minds:

"Our minds are extended in every act of perception, reaching even as far as the stars. What we see around us is in our minds but not in our brains. When we look at something, in a sense our mind touches it."

His book raises lots of questions about basic scientific beliefs and also what science knows. Turns out even some of the fixed laws of nature aren't really so fixed.

It is amazing to me what, as a people of the earth, we *don't* know. Not knowing is a good thing - it means we are free to explore, journey for ourselves, discover our own truth. I'm all for not knowing.

Religions don't know anything about god, source, creator, spirit - absolutely nothing. The experience of the divine is personal - not institutional. It is an experience of the heart, soul, spirit - it is not of the mind. Religion is philosophy - mind based.

Science is based on *laws* that are mostly *theories* - and some of those theories are starting to look a little shaky.

And, yet, whether a religious or a scientific fundamentalists - they are trapped in very old thoughts and theories - in dogma. If there is anything at all to any one of the many field theories, it is clear we have moved on as a people. We have evolved despite an anchor tied to our creativity.

It amazes me how much religion and science have in common. They both came out of the same past and they are both stuck there. It's amazing they think "they know *the* truth."

What's more amazing is that most of us think they do, too.

Energy

We all talk a lot about energy. I decided to see if I could figure out what it is. So, I started with science. I wanted to understand how electricity works - that's pretty common "energy."

Well, as it turns out, nobody knows how electricity works. Now, there are a lot of theories, most based on magnetism. So, I started researching magnetism. Turns out nobody knows how it works either. Another theory. Those theories lead me to gravity - the force that keeps us from floating off to Mars or someplace. You guessed it - another theory.

I was actually very surprised. I've heard those words my whole life and I assumed somebody, somewhere a long time ago had figured out what something that basic *is*. It's all based on theories.

From Wikipedia: "Electric charge is the physical property of matter that causes it to experience a force when close to other electrically charged matter." Great, but what *is* it? I know Wikipedia may not be an iron clad source - I looked a few other places, too. I can find out how electricity is manipulated, created and used. I can't find out what it is. As I said earlier, same goes with magnetism and gravity.

Changing lanes - science also doesn't know what energy beats our hearts. Again, they know a lot about hearts and I could bore you with some detailed information. What they don't seem to know is what the energy *is* that beats my heart and keeps me alive so I can write this book.

One more example. Science also doesn't know what the energy is that breathes me. They know a lot about my lungs and electrical (there's that word again) impulses in my body, etc. I'm interested in what is the basic energy that breathes me.

If anybody reading this has discovered scientific information about what it is, please let me know.

So, I go to spirituality. Source, the universal energy, unconditional love, the field and other words you can add. It's a real shame that science and spirit can't sit down, have a drink together and get to know each other.

Here's my theory: It breathes me, spirit breaths me - and, beats my heart - and, keeps me on this planet - and, is in every atom in my body and everyplace else in all the universes that are, were or ever will be. Now there's a theory of everything. I doubt I'll be hearing from the Nobel Committee, though.

Energy - The Great Mystery

I've been doing more research on energy. The reason I keep coming back to this subject is to help my rational mind understand that there is absolutely no difference in the energy of the human mind/body and the energy of gravity, magnetism or strong and weak nuclear energy - called the *four fundamentals* by scientists.

In the words of Richard Feynman (1918 - 1988), a celebrated physics teacher and Nobel Laureate: *"It is important to realize that in physics today, we have no knowledge of what energy is."* I added the emphasis.

It took me a while to find this quote. I think that's a really, really important statement. So, if modern physics has "no knowledge of what energy is", that means it's a mystery.

OK, so what's the difference between that energy mystery and the energy mystery of how your mind and your thoughts affect your body and your world? Why do we sort of accept all these scientific theories and discount the spiritual, mind/body, field of all possibility theories? There is a serious disconnect here.

There is also a mysterious energy that beats my heart and breathes me. Modern medicine has no idea what that energy "is."

I came across some other information on my web search - all from what I consider to be reputable sources. Science believes that whatever caused the original big bang -

another mystery - all the energy that is in the universe today was unleashed. A finite amount of energy came into being all at once. The *theory* is that no new energy is ever added - it's called the *conservation of energy* theory.

This from *Scientific American*, June, 2010: "Energy can neither be created nor destroyed. This principle, called *conservation of energy*, is one of our most cherished laws of physics." I added the emphasis.

So, the scientific *theory* is that from a mysterious big bang all energy was created - and, we don't know what that energy *is*. From there scientists postulate all sorts of theories. When you get down to the basics, they have a lot of theories because they don't have a clue what's going on. Just to be clear - that means scientists don't know what gravity, magnetism, electricity or nuclear energy *is*.

OK, I'm not beating up on scientists - you all keep thinking and theorizing about it. My point is - it's a mystery. Just like the mind/body connection, manifestation from thoughts, psychic phenomena, intuition, imagination, dreams, you fill in the rest - are mysteries.

If we are going to honor scientific mysteries, then let's also honor what I'm calling spiritual mysteries. *Both* the scientific and the spiritual mysteries are in the area of the occult or hidden aspects of this dimension we are temporarily inhabiting.

We live in a totally magical, mysterious world. That seems to be the only fact I've been able to find so far.

The Holographic Universe

The Holographic Universe by Michael Talbot is a very important book. Here Talbot presents a whole new way to consider our world, based on the work of many others and on his own intuitive guidance. This book shifted me in major ways. Here are some of the main ideas presented in the book.

Remember Princess Leia in Star Wars? Artoo Detoo projects her image so Luke can see the message she is sending him. The image is a hologram, a three dimensional picture made with the aid of a laser. Some scientists now believe the universe itself is a kind of giant hologram - an illusion - no more or less real than the image of Princess Leia.

Said another way, there is evidence to suggest our world and everything in it are also only projections from a level of reality so beyond our own it is literally beyond both space and time.

A little history and a little science. I'll keep it short and simple. Niels Bohr discovered what was termed *non-locality* or *entanglement* - once subatomic particles are in contact, they remain forever influenced by each other instantaneously over any time and distance. Einstein rejected this theory since he didn't believe information could travel faster than the speed of light. Alain Aspect later demonstrated that particles could travel faster than the speed of light and he demonstrated that at the lowest level of matter, things are interconnected.

David Bohm believed separateness is an illusion - particles are not individual entities, but are actually extensions of the same fundamental something. He did not believe an objective "hard" reality exists. Rather information is enfolded - stored - in quantum waves. He used the hologram as a model to explain his theories.

Bohm considered the universe a giant information headquarters of "unbroken wholeness," in which everything in the universe is already present in some invisible domain beyond time and space - a field of all possibility - to be called forth and made manifest when necessary. A sort of cosmic storehouse of "All That Is."

Separate from Bohn, but at the same time Karl Pribram, a neuroscientist, came to the conclusion that the human brain uses quantum waves, like a hologram, to store vast quantities of information. Our brains read this information and from this create the three-dimensional world.

From these ideas, Talbot theorized the whole of the universe was one giant inseparable organism. The "all in the small" - like the hologram - each tiny portion of the encoded information contains the whole of the image. All matter exists in a vast web of connection.

We are One. Most of us feel that to be true. Seems some scientists are coming to the same conclusion.

The holographic model of the universe explains some other, non scientific, things. These include telepathy, precognition, mystical feelings of oneness with the universe and psychokinesis, the ability of the mind to move objects. Is science meeting spirit?

The paranormal itself doesn't fit into the current scientific view of the world. So, most scientists discount it, although many, many well conducted experiments have validated it. These paranormal activities can be explained by the model of a holographic universe, but cannot be explained by the currently accepted view.

These new ideas are extremely controversial, although many scientists do embrace them in part. It's important to remember scientists are people with prejudices, pre-conceived notions, etc. who are not always as objective as we may believe. Also remember people are addicted to their beliefs. When you try to change someone's beliefs, they act like an addict. The concepts in this book are new ideas being born into the scientific community. It might take a while.

I have just given a very high level summary of the book. For those of you interested in this subject, it contains lots of details of experiments and other evidence to support the basic theory of a holographic universe - all with sort of a spiritual twist. Here is a collection of the thoughts and theories of most of the out of the box thinkers of recent times.

Reading this book (I've read it twice and still pick it up and read random pages) expands my logical, thinking mind - it helps me realize how little we actually "know". Mostly I think I like it because science and spirituality are somewhat intertwined in all these thoughts. Bohm's "field of all possibilities" is basic Eastern thought and very ancient. That's just one example. You'll find lots of places where the two worlds meet in these pages.

The Source Field Investigations

The Source Field Investigations by David Wilcox discusses how our destinies on earth are being guided by a hidden intelligence - a living energy field - the Universe - the Source Field. "As above, so below" is ancient wisdom. Is mind an energetic phenomenon that travels through empty space? Here is a sample of the new thoughts presented in this book.

Hypnosis accesses the subconscious mind where commands are obeyed as if the subconscious were accustomed to taking orders. Cleve Backster found through his experiments every living thing is intimately attuned to its environment - when any plant suffered stress, all life forms in the area seemed to share the pain. He concluded every living thing in nature is listening to everything else - including us.

If all living things are in tune, perhaps our minds screen out most of the information for our own sanity. It has been proven that human consciousness has direct access to events in the future.

The pineal gland located in the center of our brain was thought by the ancients to be the seat of the soul - transformation - awakening - rebirth. The teachings of the ancient mystery schools have been associated with this "eye of wisdom" - the third eye. Electromagnetic (cell phones, etc.) energy may interfere with information in the Source Field.

Discovering Wisdom
When We Realize We Are Love - Everything Shifts

What if we are all sharing the same mind? There have been discussions about the hive mind - as new ideas are introduced into the energy field, they suddenly become available to everyone - the phenomenon of simultaneous discovery. Sheldrake believed we are all accessing a common databank of information - the concept of a shared mind. Experiments have shown the mind is not confined to linear time.

Experiments have proven if you are having trouble concentrating and someone else in a remote location tries to help you think, then soon you will be able to focus much better. There appears to be a parallel reality - on some level. Can we improve the lives of others by improving ourselves?

Lucid dreaming is waking up in your dream, being conscious you are dreaming and able to change the outcome of your dream. A direct experience of the Source Field may be similar to lucid dreaming.

Many studies have been conducted on the power of thought. An example - many people meditating on peace reduces the crime rate. Does this work because we are all sharing the same mind? By focusing on positive attitudes in your own life you are helping to reduce war, suffering and death. Might love be the key to solving many problems? What if the rules of the dream world do apply to the physical world?

It appears we have an energetic duplicate. Our DNA is somehow interfacing with an energy field that has remained largely unknown to Western scientists, and which leaves behind a phantom which can easily be measured. It's like a perfect hologram of your physical body which is correct down to the tiniest cell. We assume our energetic duplicate is not dying when our physical body ceases - it carries over from one alleged lifetime to another and brings our memories along with it.

1980 - Roger Lewin "Is Your Brain Really Necessary?" He studied people who had almost no brain tissue left yet had normal IQs.

Fritz-Albert Popp concluded the ability of DNA to store light was a key - all living things are constantly emitting photons. Many other experiments with humans and light are discussed.

Everyone has experienced being around people who are an energy drain - some call them energy vampires. It reinforces the idea that your energy is a finite thing that can be taken from you. There is an *infinite* energy in the Source Field once you learn how to access it by making your thoughts more coherent. That's why many ancient teachings stress meditation.

What if cancer can be traced back to a loss of light, of energy. We do appear to have the power to heal others with thoughts and perhaps our light energy.

The Source Field is changing - pushing us toward a higher coherence and rearranging our genetic code in favorable ways. Happiness levels worldwide have increased.

The above is a high level summary of Part One of this book. At the end of the book Wilcox concludes 2012 ushered in the golden age and all his discussions lend credence to his belief.

The Field

The Field, The Quest for the Secret Force of the Universe by Lynne McTaggart is a summary of some of the groundbreaking work that has been done by scientists - some would say on the edge of research.

In *The Field* Lynn McTaggart tells the story of an emerging scientific story - one of unity where the parts affect the whole every moment. What if a quantum field holds us all together in its invisible web? What if we are in constant and instantaneous interaction with our environment?

This book is filled with scientific breakthroughs, mostly discovered in the 1970s and 1980s, by largely unknown frontier scientific explorers. It was first published in 2001 - the last update in 2008. Since its first publication more recent studies have corroborated and/or expanded some of these new - even radical ideas. What if, as some of these studies indicate, consciousness is central to shaping our world. It seems the ancient wisdom teachings are meeting quantum physics. How cool is that!

The old (and some would say, current) scientific world view saw the world as a machine and our bodies as simply another machine in a disjointed, separate universe. These views turned scientist into mechanics - no room for spiritual or metaphysical phenomenon.

Enter quantum physics. When the world was investigated at the level of the tiniest bit of matter, it was discovered that our world isn't made up of matter at all - it isn't even a thing (in the way we normally think of that word). The world appears to be made of sometimes one thing, sometimes something quite different and can be many possible things at the same time. The sub atomic particles these scientists were studying appeared to have no meaning in isolation, but only in relationship to everything else. It appeared this newly discovered universe could only be understood as a dynamic web of interconnection. Things once in contact remained always in contact through all space and time. Actually, time and space as we normally think of those terms, appears not to exist at all. At this point in their research, some of the scientist doing this work turned to classic philosophical teachings in an effort to understand what they were seeing.

One of the other worldview changing discoveries was that the observer can change the observed. Subatomic particles existed in all possible states until disturbed by us - by observing or measuring - at which point they would settle down - oftentimes into what the observer expected them to settle in to. Our observation, our human consciousness, was utterly central to this process of subatomic flux. Scientists realized that the observers where somehow a key here, but didn't quite know how to account for that variable. Up to this point science held that human experimenters were on the outside looking in. Now, it appeared this long held belief may not be true.

Some scientists began working with the concept of the Zero Point Field - the microscopic vibrations in the space between things - our universe may be a sea of energy - one vast quantum field. If this is true, everything is connected to everything else - like some invisible web.

They next discovered that we humans are made of the same basic material - we are packets of quantum energy - constantly exchanging information with the field. We literally resonate with our world! These scientists demonstrated that there may be such a thing as a life force flowing through the universe - what has been called the collective consciousness or, as theologians have termed it, the Spirit.

This provided a plausible explanation of all those areas that over the centuries mankind has had faith in but no solid evidence of or adequate accounting for, from the effectiveness of alternative medicine and even prayer to life after death. They offered us, in a sense, a science of philosophy.

It appears that what we do and think matters - in fact, is critical in creating our world. Human beings were no longer separate from each other. It was no longer us and them. We were no longer at the periphery of our universe - on the outside looking in. We could take our place back in the center of our world.

The Field is the story of this scientific revolution in the making. The summary I have offered here is a very high level overview - mostly taken from the preface and prologue of the book. I have read this book twice. I'm fascinated by the details of the many scientific studies McTaggart describes here. I have found it helped my rational, thinking mind to let go a little - relax a little more - around the metaphysical ideas of how this world works.

The following are my thoughts, not a part of the book:

To me this book is truly about science meets spirit. It will be interesting to see how long it takes for these experiments and these ideas to become mainstream science.

In the 3rd century the Diamond Net of Indra from the Buddhist tradition talks of the interconnectedness of the universe. When I read about this Buddhist teaching, it sure sounds a lot like the Zero Point Field. And, the Wheel turns.

Final Note: These ideas are presented in a really good DVD - *The Living Matrix, a Film on the New Science of Healing*. This film features Lynne McTaggart, Bruce Lipton, Marilyn Schlitz, among many others. Check it out.

Truth

Say not, "I have found *the* truth," but rather, "I have found *a* truth." - Kahlil Gibran

I have been reading Kahlil Gibran (1883 - 1931) for years and have learned a lot from his writings. So, "*the*" truth versus "*a*" truth. Big difference. Think about wars - many based on religious and/or political differences - what if this simple, basic truth had been understood and honored? We each have our own truth. My truth may not be true for you. Your truth may not be true for anyone else. Isn't that the greatest thing?

Diversity. We are each free beings. We can choose. Wouldn't it be pretty amazing if we all simply honored each other's right to choose. Actually, how about we celebrate our right to choose. At our core we are one - god - source - creator. *And*, we are free to choose our own path in this dimension - in this lifetime. Lots of choices bubbling up from the same core.

Sounds all spiritual and new age-y - right? Ground it. Bring it home. Your significant other sees the world differently than you. You both do not share the same basic values or beliefs. Who's right? You both are. Now, how you ultimately negotiate your relationship might be interesting and challenging. Accepting and honoring each other would be a cornerstone to success.

Similar example with your boss, your parents, your children. Your country, your religion from childhood.

Nobody's right. Different views. Different opinions. Why argue? Why not simply accept different views?

I'll end with more Gibran: "For the vision of one man lends not its wings to another man."

Intuition

"The intuitive mind is a sacred gift and the rational mind is a faithful servant. We have created a society that honors the servant and has forgotten the gift." - Albert Einstein

You are naturally intuitive - you may or may not *consciously* utilize this natural gift. Intuition is at work in our thoughts. It's as though we can process thinking and intuiting at the same time - or perhaps they are two sides of the same coin? Aha moments. Leaps of logic. Your sixth sense.

In early 2012 the Office of Naval Research announced the US Navy would spend $3.85 million over a four year period to study how intuition works. Their goal is to offer insight into the scientific basis of intuition, a concept many in the general public confuse with the supernatural. "There is a growing body of anecdotal evidence, combined with solid research efforts, that suggests intuition is a critical aspect of how we humans interact with our environment and how, ultimately, we make many of our decisions," Ivy Estabrooke, a program manager at the Office of Naval Research, said. "The whole goal of this research endeavor is to determine if we can develop techniques to measurably improve intuition."

Some people define intuition as acquired knowledge without the use of reason. Some see it as divine or spiritual guidance or knowing. Einstein believed it was a "sacred gift."

I expect the US Navy will discover it is actually very easy to "measurably improve intuition." I participated in a 4 day workshop a few years ago that certainly measurably improved my intuition.

If you are interested in improving your own intuition, it is a matter of intention and practice - and, not the least bit difficult. I'm sure there are many teachers who work in this area. I highly recommend *The Intuitive Heart* by Henry Reed, Ph.D. and Brenda English.

I wonder how it would change our lives and our world if we all lived from the place of our sixth sense all the time, rather than in isolated moments? If we learned to honor the "sacred gift" as much as we now honor the "faithful servant?"

The Conscious Universe

The Conscious Universe, The Scientific Truth of Psychic Phenomena by Dean Radin, Ph.D. is packed with details of real scientific studies into the area of psychic phenomena. Dr. Radin presents us with proof of what most people consider new age mumbo jumbo.

Noetic science is the branch of science that investigates the role of consciousness in the physical world and, ultimately, the nature of reality. The theory that psychic phenomenon (psi) are real has been investigated by serious, rigorous scientific methods for over 100 years.

Psi phenomena fall into two general categories. The first involves perceiving objects or events beyond the range of the ordinary senses. The second is mentally causing action at a distance. In both categories, it seems that intention, the mind's will, can do things that - according to prevailing scientific theories - it isn't supposed to be able to do.

Psi has been shown to exist in thousands of experiments - an immense amount of evidence has been accumulated. There are disagreements over how to interpret the evidence, but the fact is that virtually all scientists who have studied the evidence, including the hard-nosed skeptics, now agree that something interesting is going on that merits scientific attention.

The experiments have investigated various forms of telepathy, clairvoyance, precognition, psychic healing and psychokinesis. The evidence is so well established researchers today no longer conduct "proof-oriented" experiments. Rather they focus on "process-oriented' questions like, What influences psi performance? and How does it work?

It is clear the results of the experiments are not due to chance, selective reporting, variations in experimental quality or design flaws. They have been independently replicated by competent, conventionally trained scientists at well known academic, industrial, and government supported laboratories worldwide for more than a century, and the effects are consistent with human experiences reported throughout history and across all cultures.

Few scientists are aware that any scientifically valid case can be made for psi, and fewer still realize the cumulative evidence is highly persuasive. One reason is the evidence has been suppressed and ridiculed by a relatively small group of highly skeptical philosophers and scientists.

Scientists are also human, the process of evaluating scientific claims is not as pristinely rational or logical as the general public believes. Some scientists continue to defend outmoded and inaccurate worldviews. The scientific controversy has had very little to do with the evidence itself and very much to do with the psychology, sociology and history of science. Psi threatens the very core assumptions of science.

If psychic experiences were any other form of curious natural phenomena, they would have been adopted long ago by the scientific mainstream on the basis of the evidence alone.

The eventual acceptance of psi is inevitable - acceptance is growing.

These phenomena present profound challenges to many aspects of science, philosophy and religion. Science must reconsider basic assumptions about space, time, mind and matter. Philosophers will rekindle the debate over the role of consciousness in the physical world. Theologians will reconsider the concept of divine intervention, as some phenomena previously considered to be miracles will probably become subject to scientific understanding.

A major shift in worldview.

These reconsiderations are long overdue. An exclusive focus on what might be called "the outer world" has led to a grievous split between the private world of human experience and the public world as described by science. There is every reason to expect that the same methods that gave us a better understanding of galaxies and genes will also shed light on experiences described by mystics throughout history.

Here you will find serious science with very detailed descriptions of the scientific methods employed in the various experiments, the critics' positions and a discussion of meta analysis - the way results are analyzed. The Notes and References sections are extensive.

Dean Radin, Ph.D., is senior scientist at the Institute of Noetic Sciences (IONS). He's held appointments at Princeton University, the University of Edinburgh, and several Silicon Valley think tanks, and produced cutting-edge parapsychological research for AT&T, Contel, SRI International and the U.S. government.

Entangled Minds

Entangled Minds, Extrasensory Experiences In a Quantum Reality by Dean Radin is a serious, hard core book setting forth scientific experiments in this field. First are some of the major areas of research discussed and then I conclude with some of my thoughts after having read this book.

Across many disciplines in science, basic laws or rules are changing with new discoveries. Such as:

Cosmologists, the people who study the cosmos, the stars, think they have accidentally overlooked 96% of the universe, the so called 'dark' energy.

Molecular biologists, who until recently regarded large segments of the genome as 'junk DNA' because no one knew what it was good for now think it may not be junk at all.

Neuroscientists always thought that brain neurons did not regenerate - now they know neurons do regenerate. The plasticity of the brain is much greater than previously thought. In 1980 a case was reported in *Science* where a young man was found to have virtually no brain with an IQ of 126, an honors graduate in mathematics - a normal guy.

Cosmologists believe now that black holes are a type of hologram, or an interference in patterns in space time. They have no idea how or why it works.

Quantum theories abound and are changing rapidly. Particles that are separated appear to continue to be entangled. If you affect one the other one instantaneously is affected in a like way. No matter how far away it is. It's like magic. These experiments are now 'old hat'. No one knows how it works, just that it does.

Despite everyday appearances, we might be living within a holistic, deeply interconnected reality. To be clear, these speculations are being proposed by traditional physicists, not by starry-eyed new agers or mystics.

Can two human beings become entangled? The main part of this book is putting forth experiments and theories over time, both of psi and quantum physicists to show that psi is real because of entangled minds. Radin makes a very convincing case that both psi is real and that quantum physicists are slowly, reluctantly proving it.

It has also been discovered that the observer changes the observed. Lots of very technical data and experiments and quantum theory in this book support that. It is an accepted fact. In other words, *reality* is somehow created by the observation of *itself.* "We now know that fundamental properties of the world are not determined before they are observed."

Quantum reality is holistic, and as such any attempt to study its individual pieces will give an incomplete picture. Consider - every possible outcome is possible until it is observed. As observers we have a very important role in the world.

So, something unaccounted for is connecting otherwise isolated objects (or humans).

Radin contends that psi is the human experience of the entangled universe.

In ancient times, lasting for tens of thousands of years - this could be called the Age of Magic or Spirit - reality was imagined to exist in cycles. This was inferred from the rhythms observed in the stars, the seasons, the days and the lifecycles of all living creatures. The concept of mind was associated with soul, a spark of the divine presence within us. Psi in ancient times was accepted as normal.

Next came the Industrial age, with its material clocklike view of the world of parts. We are now in the Information age of the computer. What's next. The ages are passing very quickly as compared to the many thousands of years of the age of Magic or Spirit.

It appears to some that the discoveries in quantum physics are returning us to the age of Magic and Spirit, with more information.

Some experiments have shown that observation *retroactively* influences quantum events. David Bohm, an Einstein protégé, believes there is a deeper reality than the one presented by our senses - he calls it the implicate order - an undivided holistic realm where everything is fully enfolded or entangled with everything else - even across time.

Brain research and theories say that the synapse mechanism produces a *cloud of potentials* in our brain in trillions of locations all the time. The brain is observing these potentials. The conscious mind directs all this into focused awareness. It acts as a filter - it must make decisions. It sustains what is familiar. It is theorized that one person's cloud of potentials can affect another person. The waves are one.

The universe could be a vast web of particles, which remain in contact with one another over any distance in "no time." All of physical reality is a single quantum system.

"At a level of reality deeper than the ordinary senses can grasp, our brains and minds are in intimate communion with the universe."

At some level our minds/brains are already coexistent with other people's minds, distant objects and everything else - we are one.

Psychic experiences are reframed not as mysterious powers of the mind but as momentary glimpses of the entangled fabric of reality. Quantum entanglement does not imply that signals pass between, but that separate systems are correlated.

Imagine that our mind/brain is sensitive to the dynamic state of the entire universe. The unconscious mind is always scanning - the universe - it alerts your conscious mind - a gut feeling - imagination - dreams.

We are always connected - to each other and to everything. No information transfer needs to take place because there are no separate parts.

I read this book looking for information about how astrology works. How can the planets mirror human life here on earth? The earliest archeological finds show astrology was ancient at that time. So, no one knows how long humans have believed the heavens are in accord with life here on earth. Radin makes a very convincing, *scientific* case for psi. He also gave me some food for thought about how astrology works:

The universe could be a vast web of particles, which remain in contact with one another over any distance in "no time." All of physical reality is a single quantum system. "At a level of reality deeper than the ordinary senses can grasp, our brains and minds are in intimate communion with the universe."

"Imagine our mind/brain is sensitive to the dynamic state of the entire universe. The unconscious mind is always scanning - the universe - it alerts your conscious mind - a gut feeling - imagination - dreams."

Wisdom or Knowledge or Information?

"Where is the wisdom we have lost in knowledge? Where is the knowledge we have lost in information?" - T. S. Eliot (1888 - 1965)

We hear a lot about this being the information age. Technology is making information available at warp speed across the globe. We are creating data bases for all kinds of things. A Google search gives me information concerning every conceivable area of interest. All good. Let's remember, the information may be accurate or inaccurate, complete or incomplete. At this point, it is simply raw information.

What is knowledge and how does information become knowledge? Here's one definition of knowledge: facts, information, and skills acquired by a person through experience or education; the theoretical or practical understanding of a subject.

OK. Now, how do I gain knowledge, as opposed to a falsehood? By writing this I am attempting to transfer knowledge I've gained to you. How do you know it's true? Am I to be believed? So, you can see turning information into knowledge is tricky.

So far in this process we have raw information - not truth in any absolute sense - just raw information. It gets picked up, absorbed by the mind of a human being who takes the raw information and transforms it through some unknown alchemical process into knowledge - something the human being *knows*.

Garbage in, garbage out! In our world where we are inundated with information from so many sources, our first task is to question the accuracy or validity of the information. If our raw information is flawed, our knowledge is flawed.

Let's assume we have good information and our mysterious, alchemical brain process has combined it with other good information and we have transformed it into knowledge, untainted by our own biases? That's all a stretch, but for now we will assume it is possible.

Now we have knowledge.

What is wisdom and how does knowledge become wisdom? Wikipedia: "A basic definition of wisdom is the judicious application of knowledge. . . . Nicholas Maxwell, a contemporary philosopher in the United Kingdom, advocates that academia ought to *alter its focus from the acquisition of knowledge to seeking and promoting wisdom*, which he defines as *the capacity to realize what is of value in life, for oneself and others.* He teaches that new knowledge and technological know-how *increase our power to act which, without wisdom, may cause human suffering and death as well as human benefit.*" [Emphasis added]

So, it seems without wisdom, all the information and knowledge everywhere and everywhen isn't of much value to us - may actually be harmful to us? I believe this is the core issue in our world today. A whole bunch of information and knowledge and very little wisdom. We *can* act before we have stopped to consider whether it's in our best interest *to* act.

Socrates (469 BC - 399 BC) got it. He had a lot of skepticism towards his own self-made knowledge. He felt his skepticism left him free to receive true wisdom as a spontaneous insight or inspiration. Sounds a lot like intuition? So, he didn't value his knowledge as much as his inspirations or his intuition.

Albert Einstein believed: "The intuitive mind is a sacred gift and the rational mind is a faithful servant. We have created a society that honors the servant and has forgotten the gift."

David Bohm felt: "The ability to perceive or think differently is more important than the knowledge gained." "Perceive" - also sounds a lot like intuition?

So, wisdom?

First, I must discover what's true for me. Of all the information out there and all the knowledge - what's true? We may each find different truths. I have spent a lifetime gathering information and knowledge - the pieces to the puzzle of life. I don't have all the pieces yet and I may never have them all. It seems my life is an ever changing picture - the pieces that fit last year may not fit into this year's view.

Next I listen to my intuition - the small voice inside - of all the choices available to me what choices are in my highest good and the highest good of all? Then I act.

Intuition is an important component of wisdom. It is the ability to know something directly without any knowledge or analytical reasoning. Intuition joins the conscious and unconscious parts of our mind. Another mysterious aspect of who we are. What is it? Where does it come from? How does it work? No one knows. Do you see? Lots of mystery and magic between information and wisdom.

Finally, wisdom is gained through the act of choice making. It really doesn't matter so much whether we make the right or wrong choice. We'll do both as life unfolds. What matters is we are aware of the outcome of our choices and we adjust our future choices in light of this new information gained from our experience. All the while, intuition is there - ready to help us *know*, without knowledge. To help wisdom blossom.

The Biology of Belief

The Biology of Belief, Unleashing the Power of Consciousness, Matter & Miracles by Bruce H. Lipton, Ph.D. helps us understand the mind/body connection. Following is a summary and excerpts from this very important book.

Bruce Lipton is a former medical school professor and research scientist. The basic premise of this book is that our genes and DNA do *not* control our biology, rather DNA is controlled by signals from outside the cell, including messages from our positive and negative thoughts. Our bodies can be changed as we retrain our thinking.

I believe you will find valuable information in the following summary. More pieces of the puzzle.

In 1985, while working as a cell biologist and medical school professor, Bruce Lipton had a life-changing realization. It is the single cell's "awareness" of the environment, not its genes, that sets into motion the mechanisms of life.

Just like the cell, our life is determined not by our genes but by our beliefs. He realized he could change his life by changing his beliefs - he could move from victim beliefs to a position of being a co-creator of his destiny.

In 1990 H. F. Nijhout pointed out that the notion that genes control biology had been repeated for so long everyone had forgotten it was a hypothesis - a theory - never proven. He said: "When a gene product is needed, a signal from its environment, not an emergent property of the gene itself, activates expression of that gene." In other words, when it comes to genetic control, "It's the environment, stupid."

The human genome project was begun in the late 1980s. At the beginning scientists expected to find approximately 120,000 genes, instead they actually found approximately 25,000. Genes don't explain why humans are at the top of the evolutionary ladder. There isn't much difference between human genes and primate genes.

The Magical Membrane. The cell's membrane which interacts with its environment is the mechanism by which belief affects biology. Integral Membrane Proteins (IMPs) embed themselves into the cell's membrane. These IMPs are so important that a new scientific field of study has come into being - signal transduction scientists study the complex information pathways that lie between the membrane's reception of environmental signals and the activation of the cell's behavior proteins.

"The membrane is a liquid crystal semiconductor with gates and channels." The definition of a computer chip is: "A chip is a crystal semiconductor with gates and channels." The cell membrane was indeed a structural and functional equivalent of a silicon chip.

The next big insight was that both cells and computers are programmable. And, that the program lies outside the computer/cell. Biological behavior and gene activity are dynamically linked to information from the environment, which is downloaded into the cell. This means we are the drivers of our own biology.

The New Physics. Biologists stick to the physical world of Newton and ignore the invisible quantum world of Einstein, in which matter is actually made up of energy and there are no absolutes. Many alternative healing modalities are based on the belief that energy fields are influential in controlling our physiology and our health.

It was discovered that atoms are made out of invisible energy not tangible matter. Matter can simultaneously be defined as a solid (particle) and as an immaterial force field (wave). The Universe is one indivisible, dynamic whole in which energy and matter are so deeply entangled it is impossible to consider them as independent elements.

Despite these discoveries in physics, biologists and the medical fields continue to view the body as a machine, discounting the invisible energy component. They have ignored the role energy plays in health and in disease. Rather than seeing the human body as a holistic feedback system, they continue to view it as a linear, mechanistic flow.

This leads to a new way to view medicine generally and pharmaceuticals in particular. Why do drugs come with pages of potential dangers? The current system treats one isolated health issue, rather than viewing the system as a whole - mind, body, spirit. A disturbance in any one of the three can affect the other two.

The major reason why medical energy research has been all but ignored is money - a trillion-dollar pharmaceutical industry - looking for magic pills. In reality helping one issue, many times only to cause another. Using drugs to silence a body's symptoms enables us to ignore personal involvement - it provides a vacation from personal responsibility.

There are no serious research funds available for studying energy based medicine. Ironically, many of the diagnostic tools used are energy based.

We already "know" all organisms, including humans, communicate and read their environment by evaluating energy fields. Because we humans are so dependent on spoken and written language, we have neglected our energy sensing communication system. A lack of use has led to atrophy.

Biology and Belief. Thoughts, the mind's energy, directly influence how the physical brain controls the body's physiology. Harnessing the power of your mind can be more effective than drugs you have been programmed to believe you need. Energy is a more effective means of affecting matter than chemicals.

We have all been conditioned to a lesser or greater extent. Conscious mind free will can override the subconscious programming.

Placebo research is extensive and has proven over and over that placebos affect cures as often, if not more often, than conventional treatments. Sugar pills, operations where the patient's skin was cut, but nothing else done, etc. It is the belief effect. The patient believed they were cured.

If positive thinking - believing you have been cured - is powerful. Imagine how powerful negative thoughts can be. Your beliefs act like filters on a camera, changing how you see the world. And your biology adapts to those beliefs. We hold the key to health and freedom - we can change our minds.

You can filter your life with rose colored beliefs that will help your body grow or you can use a dark filter that turns everything black and makes your body/mind more susceptible to disease. You can live a life of fear or live a life of love. You have that choice.

Learning how to harness your mind to promote growth is the secret of life. It is not our genes but our beliefs that control our lives.

You are personally responsible for everything in your life, once you become aware that you are responsible for everything in your life. You can reprogram.

The Spontaneous Healing of Belief

The Spontaneous Healing of Belief, Shattering the Paradigm of False Limits by Gregg Braden is another book with the potential to expand our view of our world. I've read all of Gregg Braden's books and always walk away a different person. Here are some excerpts of his wisdom from this most interesting book.

We may think we are only observing our world - in fact, by watching we become part of what we are watching. Consciousness is a vast field and it appears there is no clear boundary between us and the rest of the universe. Ancient wisdom taught everything is connected - as energy - and, it *is*. We are participators - we live in an interactive reality. As we change - our thoughts, feelings, beliefs - the world around us changes to match our energy vibration.

The Implication: From healing disease to the length of our lives, to the success of our careers and relationships, everything that we experience as "life" is directly linked to what we believe.

The Bottom Line: To change our lives and relationships, heal our bodies, and bring peace to our families and nations requires a simple yet precise shift in the way we use our belief.

Some scientists are turning the scientific world upside down - akin to a revolution. They are discovering some of the basic facts of science are false.

Discovering Wisdom
When We Realize We Are Love - Everything Shifts

False Assumption 1: The space between "things" is empty. New discoveries now tell us that this is simply not true.

False Assumption 2: Our inner experience of feeling and belief have no effect on the world beyond our bodies. This has been proven absolutely wrong as well.

Paradigm-shattering experiments published in leading-edge peer-reviewed journals reveal that we're bathed in a field of intelligent energy that fills what used to be thought of as empty space. Additional discoveries show beyond any reasonable doubt that this field responds to us - it rearranges itself - in the presence of our heart-based feelings and beliefs. And this is the revolution that changes everything.

Since the time of Isaac Newton's "laws" of physics which were formalized in 1687, we've based what we accept as our capabilities and limits on information that is false or, at least, incomplete. Since that time science has been grounded in the belief that we are insignificant in the overall scheme of things.

It seems the world is now forcing us to rediscover who we really are - pushing us to new frontiers of consciousness. With each thought, word and action we change the world. We don't' need science to explain our world to us - our everyday lives show us how powerful we are.

Sounds too simple - and, maybe too frightening? We are at a turning point - we are discovering how the universe really works and are beginning to accept our interactive role in it.

In the Late 1990s and early 2000s, research has revealed the following facts:

Fact 1: The universe, our world, and our bodies are made of a shared field of energy that was scientifically recognized in the 20th century and is now identified by names that include the field, the quantum hologram, the mind of God, nature's mind and the Divine Matrix.

Fact 2: In the field of the Divine Matrix, "things" that have been connected physically and then separated act as if they are still linked, through a phenomenon known as *entanglement*.

Fact 3: Human DNA directly influences what happens in the Divine Matrix in a way that appears to defy the laws of time and space.

Fact 4: Human belief (and the feelings and emotions surrounding it) directly changes the DNA that affects what occurs in the Divine Matrix.

Fact 5: When we shift our beliefs about our bodies and our world, the Divine Matrix translates that change into the reality of our lives.

Do you believe you are born with the natural ability to create and modify your body and the world? If so, what *responsibility* do you have to use this power wisely? Can you accept the powerful scientific evidence that consciousness itself and your role in it are the missing links in the theories of how the world works? Heavy stuff. We're back to the big "R" word - *responsibility*.

Let's say you are ready to step up and live an awake, conscious life - ready to take responsibility for your thoughts, words and actions. Ready to realize that you create your world, as well as, *the* world. If this is the future, how do you learn to live in this way?

In 1923 Kahlil Gibran wrote: "No man can reveal to you aught but that which already lies half asleep in the dawning of your knowledge." He is telling us we can't be taught anything we don't already know. That knowing may be deep inside, not conscious.

In this book Gregg Braden's intent is to help us remember.

We are told by some that we are frail and powerless beings who live in a world where things just "happen" for no apparent reason. Conversely, most ancient wisdom tells us there is a force that lives within each of us - a power that nothing in the world can touch. A power that helps us through the difficult times which are a part of the journey of life. Which to believe? No wonder we are confused.

Which is it? Are you a fragile victim or a powerful creator with abilities you are only now beginning to understand?

The role you play in life is determined by the choices you make - *choices based on your beliefs*.

This summary is really a summary of the introduction to this book. The main part of the book deals with how to identify and change *beliefs* that are not in your highest good. You will learn to: identity beliefs that reverse disease in your body; learn the ones that create lasting, nurturing relationships in your life; and, uncover those that bring peace to your life, your family, your community, and your world.

You will learn about the language of beliefs and the feelings you have about what you believe. You will also be called to walk the bridge over the gap between the science of today and the wisdom of the past.

As Rumi (1207 - 1273) wrote: "We are the mirror, and the face in the mirror. We are the sweet cold water, and the jar that pours [the water]."

Do you have the courage to accept your role in the universe and realize you can change the world by changing yourself?

How Are You Affecting The World?

"We are all affecting the world every moment, whether we mean to or not. Our actions and states of mind matter, because we are so deeply interconnected with one another." - Ram Dass

Did you ever stop to think that everything you do, say, feel, think is affecting the entire universe? And, all people from all ages everywhere and everywhen likewise have and will affect the whole.

We hear the words - we are one. We all exist in the same field - and, that field has existed since the beginning - whenever that was. The vibration of the field or the character of the field is determined by our states of mind, our actions, our feelings. It is a composite of the energy of all beings across all times. A sort or repository. If I am angry - the vibration in the field is altered - minutely - altered. If I am filled with love - the vibration is also altered.

There have been many scientific studies showing when a new skill is learned by an animal on one side of the globe, the skill will spontaneously be expressed by animals on the other side of the world. Scientists believe this may happen due to organizing fields that have an inherent memory. This idea - morphic fields - was first proposed several years ago. It is theorized there may be some sort of collective memory specific to each species. Sound familiar?

Discovering Wisdom
When We Realize We Are Love - Everything Shifts

Carl Jung put forth the theory of the collective unconscious. The theory, in part, states we may have some communion with some divine or world mind. The collective unconscious may be a body of unconscious energy that lives forever.

Edgar Cayce, a modern prophet, spoke of the one mind. He said there is one mind and we all share it. Our individual, personal conscious mind is a part of the one mind. Today we might say the transpersonal mind - the mind has a life beyond what appears in individual persons. It is a reality in itself.

Air is transpersonal. You have your air and I have mine. And yet, air is everywhere. One large body of air we all share. Air quality these days is a big topic of discussion. There is only one air - there is only one mind. Energy quality in the mind may be comparable to air quality?

Rupert Sheldrake has developed a theory of morphic resonance. He presents a vision of transpersonal reality of mind similar to Cayce's perspective. The more people able to conceive of an idea - the easier it becomes for others to have the same idea. Data collected from 1918 to 1989 showed that IQ scores in the US have been rising for decades by 30% or more. Scientists have put forth many ideas about why this is happening. Maybe it's the field - the one mind - morphic fields?

Imagine your brain as a TV set. Imagine the broadcast airwaves to be the one mind or energy in the morphic field. Ideas are vibrational patterns in those waves. Your brain tunes into ideas that are *in the air*. The one mind is a reality in itself independent of your brain or body.

Now, mainstream science still doesn't get it. That doesn't mean the new theories are wrong. They simply haven't gained enough energy in the field quite yet. You see? We each change the field every second.

Do you want world peace, as I do? Ask yourself whether your actions, words, feelings and thoughts are peaceful or not? What energy or information are you adding to the field every day? How are you affecting the world?

Moon Beams Illuminating Science?

Astrology is based on the principle: As above, so below. In other words what's going on in the cosmos mirrors the actions of people here on earth.

A full moon occurs when the moon is 180 degrees across from the sun. In astrology we would say they are in opposition. The moon represents feelings and emotions and the sun represents vitality. In the full moon opposition they are in dynamic tension. Perhaps some people feel the pull of the sun to move more than they feel the pull of the moon to rest which could account for restless sleep? And, perhaps lack of rest could account for some of the *anecdotal* evidence of the lunar effect: increased admissions to hospitals, especially psychiatric wards, crime rates, etc.

We all know the moon affects the tides here on earth and our bodies are mostly water. So it might also make some intuitive sense that the moon affects women's monthly cycles, conception or child birth.

I was doing some research on the web looking for scientific evidence, rather than anecdotal evidence. Turns out the vast majority of scientific studies don't support the lunar effect. Some studies support the lunar effect but were discredited, a small number support the lunar effect and some studies were contradictory. I did come across the following study having to do with sleep patterns.

The following was taken in part from a recent article by Edward Snow on the web site of Astrology News Service.

Professor Christian Cajochen, a psychiatrist who studies circadian rhythms at the University of Basel in Switzerland, was having cocktails with colleagues at a local pub. The full moon had risen and was flooding their table with light.

When the conversation turned to shop talk some of the professor's colleagues complained they slept less well when the moon was full. After years of studying sleep patterns, Prof. Cajochen realized he had enough data to check out these claims and made a decision to do so the next day.

It was the researcher's intention to prove his friends wrong by disproving their hypothesis: sleep patterns are influenced by the full moon. "To my surprise I couldn't," he reportedly said.

Most scientists believe they have the physical universe pretty well figured out and moon beams don't figure in their calculations.

For his test, Prof. Cajochen used data collected *10 years earlier* for another study. Thirty-three participants between the ages of 12 and 75 were grouped based on whether the moon was new or full when they entered the laboratory for extended testing.

Results of the test are described in the journal *Current Biology*. The researchers found that those who came into the sleep laboratory during a full moon took five minutes longer to fall asleep and had 20 minutes less sleep on average. Even more significantly, test subjects spent *30 percent less time in restful deep sleep* than those who entered the lab under a different lunar phase.

By being *retrospective*, critics will find it hard to claim any experimental or selection bias of subjects or data. A simple mechanism such as increased moonlight can also be ruled out as the subjects slept in a dark room in the sleep laboratory. Neither the 33 volunteers nor the scientists conducting the tests were aware of the lunar phase at any time.

Here is one solid study clearly showing the correlation between moon phase and restful sleep. And, Prof. Cajochen set out to prove the opposite with data collected for an entirely different reason 10 years before he analyzed the data for this purpose. It took him 4 years to publish his findings because he worried what his peers in the scientific community would think of him.

Earlier in this book I discussed Rupert Sheldrake's book entitled *Science Set Free: 10 Paths to New Discovery.* In his book he shows the ways in which science is being held back by assumptions that have, over the years, hardened into dogmas. Such dogmas are not only limiting, but dangerous for the future of humanity.

I wonder what lunar effect studies would actually show if scientists were set free to have an open mind?

Is the Unseen Real?

Is the Occult - the unseen, hidden, secret, paranormal - real? Well, maybe? Many of us are interested in the occult. To me it's more about studying a deeper, spiritual reality. Studying things that can't be measured, the things hard core science may not acknowledge as real. The unseen, the mysteries of life. And, yet, aspects of our human existence that seem real.

Electricity was discovered in 1600 by William Gilbert. Well, actually he did a careful study of electricity. Studies have been found dating back to 2750 BC of fish emitting electric shocks. And, there is always lightning - it's been around for a while. Work to understand electricity continued in the 18th and 19th centuries. We now know a lot of the properties of electricity and it is surely an integral part of our lives. We take for granted that it is measurable and real. Yet, we still don't know what it or magnetism are. So, I suppose you could put it in the category of the occult?

You see? Until we can explain or see something we label it as out there, new age nonsense, woo-woo. Like electricity, once it can be explained it fits into our material view of the world. Always remember electricity and magnetism. We have absolutely no idea what they *are*.

In this section I begin with several articles concerning astrology. It is important for many reasons. First of all it can help each of us see ourselves more clearly and negotiate our way through life with more ease. Secondly, once it is accepted as real a whole new world will open up before us - an unseen world.

From there a few articles on shamanism. It, too, has stood the test of time. And, it, too, works in some unseen way.

Just to continue to expand our minds and consider wisdom from any source, I look at witchcraft and paganism. And, end up with an oracle or two just for kicks.

It has been important to me and my journey of discovery to keep an open mind and to consider all teachings, especially ancient ones. I have found great wisdom in astrology, shamanism, paganism and the ancient oracles. I am convinced we are living in some sort of energy field which is the mechanism through which all of these unseen and yet powerful teachings work.

Remember, this sounds a lot like quantum physics! So, if you can, keep an open mind - read on, pilgrim, read on.

Astrology - The Divine Science

I count astrology as one of the wisdom traditions. I've learned a lot from studying it. Lots of people think of astrology as new age craziness and discount it. When I study quantum physics and the *Field* or Deepak Chopra and the *Field of all Possibilities*, I wonder if the vibration or energy of the Field is the mechanism through which astrology works? Maybe I'll never understand the *how* of astrology. Sort of like no one understands what gravity, magnetism or electricity *is*. Those scientific mysteries are accepted. I wonder why the mystery surrounding astrology prevents it from being accepted?

Ray Grasse speaks of astrology as the Divine Science. I like that. Following is an introduction to the subject and some history.

The earliest known writing on the earth came down to us from the Sumerian civilization. A large number of stone tablets have been found from this time. They date to around 3000 BC - that's 5000 years ago. These tablets contained, among other things, lots of references to astrology. Evidence of astrology has also been found in all the major civilizations of that time. It appears to archeologists that the earliest found writing was only copies of much earlier texts. And, of course, before the invention of writing all knowledge was passed down orally. So, it really isn't known how old astrology is.

Astrology quickly developed into an incredibly complex practice. By 2000 BC the priests of the time believed there were no accidents, and that everything in the universe, people, objects and events, was connected. Astrology and astronomy were one science and astrologers were the best educated people. They were the close advisors of kings.

Astrology was taught in universities up until the 1600s when rational science took over. Isaac Newton (1642 - 1727) was a practicing astrologer, as well as many other prominent people of that era. So, from before 3000 BC through AD 1600 astrology was a well respected science. Around AD 1600 rational science gained popularity and astrology was relegated to the occult and lost credibility because it was not based on hard science.

Think about life 5000 years ago. When you looked up what did you see? Pretty much the same thing we see today. All of the ancient gods were based on observations of the stars. Mars was associated with the god of war, Venus with love and beauty. Those associations were made after much data was collected about the synchronicity of the movement of those planets with life here on earth. As above, so below.

Astrology is based on the *relationships* between the planets, the sun, the moon - the 12 zodiac signs - and, the 12 houses which represent areas of a person's life. Your birth chart is the map of your journey through this life and through many lifetimes.

So, is everything in your life predestined or do you have free will? Both. It is predestined by your soul; and you, the personality, the ego, have free will. It goes like this.

As a soul, you have lived many lifetimes and will live many more. If that statement makes you feel uncomfortable, you might consider for now simply keeping an open mind and see how you feel at the end of this little ride. As a soul, prior to your incarnation into this lifetime, you decided what you wanted to work on this time through. Your prior lifetimes, what you decided to work on and where you are going as a soul can all be seen in the chart.

As a personality, an ego living on this material earth, the chart shows your *possibilities* as you move through time during this lifetime. My Sun is in Libra, the sign of balance and relationship. That means in this lifetime I will be presented with experiences that will enable me to learn a great deal about balance and relationships. It also means I have a natural aptitude or interest in those areas. So, if I follow my desires, I'll naturally become proficient at balance and relationship. If not, then maybe next time through!

Think about it as a card game. You are dealt cards - the planets, signs and houses. You're sitting at the table with other players. And, your soul's intention for this lifetime is the game you are playing. You might think of all of that as predestination. Just don't forget - it's how *you* play your cards, how you interact with the cards other players have played, that will determine the outcome of the game. So, freewill. You are always at choice in this lifetime. The stars don't dictate, they incline. Instead of looking to astrology for answers, look to it for choices. *You* provide the answers - *you* decide how you want to play your cards. The phrase "go with the flow" comes to mind. Sometimes things in life seem so very easy, at other times those very same things feel like herding cats. Astrology can help you "go with the flow" of your soul's journey and of your evolving personality.

Psychological Astrology

Psychological astrology, or astropsychology, is the result of the cross-fertilization of the fields of astrology with depth psychology, humanistic psychology and transpersonal psychology. The horoscope is analyzed through the archetypes within astrology to gain psychological insight into an individual's psyche. Astrologer and psychotherapist Glenn Perry characterizes psychological astrology as "both a personality theory and a diagnostic tool."

Jungian legacy.

Several astrologers as well as psychologists pursued Jung's theories in their writings, teachings and practice. One of the first astrologers to combine Jungian psychology with astrology was Dane Rudhyar and his protégé, Alexander Ruperti. Rudhyar termed it "humanistic astrology," the subject of his monumental volume, *The Astrology of Personality*, published in 1936. Psychological astrology, however became firmly established in the late 20th century with the books and lectures of Liz Greene and Stephen Arroyo who were both strongly influenced by the Jungian model. In 1983, Liz Greene and Howard Sasportas, a psycho synthesis psychotherapist, founded the Centre for Psychological Astrology in London.

Meanwhile, in Switzerland, Bruno Huber & Louise Huber also developed their own method of astrological psychology, referred to as the Huber Method which was influenced by Roberto Assagioli's work with psycho synthesis. In 1962, the Hubers founded the Huber School of Astrology and their work is now taught at the Astrological Psychology Association.

Possibly the most widespread application of Jung's theories is through the Myers-Briggs Type Indicator (MBTI) assessment developed during the Second World War. CPP Inc., the publisher of the MBTI instrument, calls it "the world's most widely used personality assessment." With as many as two million assessments administered annually.

This psychometric questionnaire is designed to measure psychological preferences in how people perceive the world and make decisions. These preferences were extrapolated from the typological theories proposed by Jung and first published in his 1921 book *Psychological Types*. So the authors, Briggs and Myers, adapted Jung's four psychological types, which were based on the four elements of classical cosmology on which the zodiac, with its corresponding human character traits, was structured. Nicholas Campion comments that this is "a fascinating example of 'disguised astrology', masquerading as science in order to claim respectability."

While psychological astrology brings a transpersonal dimension and spiritual notions to psychology by linking the psyche to the Cosmos, psychological astrology is "decidedly not deterministic." Nor is an individual's everyday life ruled by malefic or benefic planets as the horoscope is considered a mere tool to help identify an individual's nature and potential for psycho-spiritual growth.

How Does Astrology Work?

I've been interested in Astrology for years. It is fascinating to me that from as long ago as humans began observing the heavens it was believed the stars affected life here on earth. This belief was a cornerstone in most civilizations in one form or another until about AD 1650 - the Age of Reason or the Age of Enlightenment. With the increased power and influence of the Church during this time, the practice of astrology in the West fell into decline. In 1666 astrology was officially banned from the Academy of Sciences in France. Astrology had a very long run - thousands of years!

In the late1960s and 1970s interest in astrology in America began to grow. Wisdom just can't be destroyed.

Astrology is the study of the cycles of the planets. Astrology doesn't claim the planets have any direct impact on individuals in any way. It works because the same force that moves the planets, also moves us. We are all a part of the universe and we all follow the same cycles and patterns. It can be difficult for us to see the patterns at work in our lives unless we have attained a very clear state of awareness. However, by observing the regular cycles of the planets, we can understand the nature of our own cycles.

Astrology is also based on the Law of Correspondences: As above, so below. As within, so without. As the universe, so the soul.

Astrology follows the Law of Alchemy - all the energies are inside us. If we suppress or deny them, they will manifest outside us. Any lessons we don't approach on a conscious level will manifest in our lives as external forces that are far more difficult to ignore. The more we try to ignore or repress these energies, the larger the disruptions become.

Finally, astrology operates on the Law of Beginning - the beginning point of a thing contains the potential that will be fulfilled during the life cycle and beyond.

This leads to the natural question of free will v. fate or determinism. If we have free will, how can the position of the planets at our birth be predictive of our lives?

We have free will and we almost never use it - not really. We tend to ride the waves of the energies at play in our lives. We are mostly on auto pilot, *not* exercising our free will.

Astrology tells us a lot about the waves of energies - the cycles. Once we are aware of the energies at play, then we are in a better position to exercise our free will - consciously interacting with the cyclical energy, rather than being mindlessly carried along on the wave.

Maybe all the people who lived in all the ages before ours just might have understood life here on earth a whole lot better than we do. I wonder?

Reference: *Astrology: Understanding the Birth Chart* by Kevin Burk, 2001

Astrology, Psychology and The Four Elements

Astrology, Psychology and The Four Elements, An Energy Approach to Astrology & Its Use in the Counseling Arts by Stephen Arroyo, M.A. nicely blends two of my favorite subjects - astrology and psychology. It's a shame astrology fell out of favor years ago. It is rich with ancient wisdom and has so much to teach us. Following are a few of the jewels of wisdom you will find in this book.

Part I - Astrology and Psychology

Astrology gets a bad rap with most people because they equate it to the sun sign columns shown in various places. Those columns are not astrology. Astrology is a very complex symbolic language.

Carl Jung understood the value of astrology. "Obviously astrology offers much to psychology, but that which the latter can contribute to its elder sister is less obvious." Jung stated that the innate psychic predisposition of an individual "seems to be expressed in a recognizable way in the horoscope." He emphasized that astrology includes the sum total of all ancient psychological knowledge. Jung also spoke of archetypes as the universal principles underlying and motivating all psychological life. Astrology is the language of symbols and is closely related to Jung's views concerning archetypes.

Almost every culture we know of had some form of astrology. This was due to their sense of unity with the cosmic environment.

Discovering Wisdom
When We Realize We Are Love - Everything Shifts

The unity of, and relation between man and the universe, is really the only assumption upon which astrology is based.

Man seems to know everything and understand nothing.

We need more of an emphasis on the whole rather than merely its parts; we need to look again at the universal principles underlying all life before we begin to tamper with nature.

L. L. Whyte: "If the whole of nature is one great system in perpetual transformation and development, the attempt to isolate any part is bound to lead to failure. . . . Man can only fully understand himself by fusing objective knowledge which is gained by observation of the whole of organic nature with the subjective knowledge of individual experience."

Jung: "Scientific education is based . . . on statistical truths and abstract knowledge and therefore imparts an unrealistic, rational picture of the world, in which the individual, as a merely marginal phenomenon, plays no role. The individual, however, as an irrational datum, is the true and authentic carrier of reality."

Joseph Campbell - the gods in myth (just like the planets in astrology) represent living forces and principles in the universe and in the lives of each of us.

Astrology is a way of understanding our fundamental nature, discovering our place in the universe, and helping us live in a creative and fulfilling way.

In astrology every individual is considered a whole and unique expression of universal principles, patterns and energies. The Zodiac was considered by the ancients as the "soul of nature" - that which gives form and order to life.

The birth chart is the graph through which the cosmos (or larger whole) enables us to understand its energies and rhythms, particularly how they operate within each individual.

No matter what label may be used to designate these universal principles, whether archetypes, essences, or formative principles, the fact remains that such forces exist in the universe and influence each of us both from within and from without.

Perhaps man can never express in words the transcendent realities of the cosmos. Still we can make use of this symbolic language if we consider it to represent universal patterns, principles and forces, however transcendent such factors may be.

The entire universe is one whole system - within the great whole there are lesser wholes whose structures, patterns and functions correspond completely to those of the greater whole. Compare a single atom to the solar system.

By studying the cycles and patterns in the greater whole (the planets) we can learn about the cycles and patterns within man himself.

If indeed the universe is one whole, how can anything cause anything else?

James F. T. Bugenthal: "To make a statement about a distant galaxy is to make a statement about oneself. To propose a 'law' of the action of mass and energy is to offer a hypothesis about one's way of being in the world. To write a description of micro-organisms on a slide is to set forth an account of human experience. . . . any statement we make about the world 'out there' is inevitably, inescapably a statement about our theory of ourselves 'in here'."

The value of astrology is in the application of this knowledge of the universal laws in our individual lives.

Dane Rudhyar - basic premise - existence manifests at all levels in terms of wholes, organized fields of interdependent activities. Astrology is man's most complete language of the form, structure and rhythm of functional wholes.

Rudhyar: "Each time anything individualizes out from the whole, it remains part of the whole. . . . This organic whole - the individual person - is essentially no different from the almost infinitely greater and vaster organized Whole, which we call the universe."

Rudhyar - the point is to be able to see where everything that happens at any time fits into the total pattern or structure of your existence. Showing man the meaningfulness of his life is the most important thing that astrology can do.

Humanistic astrology - changes from knowing what kind of problem a person has to what kind of person has a problem.

Part II - The Four Elements

Astrology has many symbols in its language. The four elements is one of many of the energies at play in a human being - one of many symbols an astrologer seeks to understand. It is, however, integral to all other symbols.

Analyzing the four elements is an energy approach to analyzing the birth chart. The basic foundation upon which astrology is based is energy - all physical and mental life is a manifestation of energy.

Astrology indicates that certain specific energies and energy patterns are established at birth and continue to operate throughout life. But what any individual will do with these energies and how he will direct them reflects free will.

Basic building blocks - these four elements interweave and combine to form all matter. At death the elements dissociate and return to their primal state. Life itself holds the elements together. The elements are fire, earth, air and water.

All four are in every person although each person is consciously attuned to some types of energy more than others.

In addition, each of the four elements manifests in three vibrational modalities. When we combine the four elements with the three modalities, we have twelve primary patterns of energy which are called the zodiacal signs. The signs have been called energy fields, archetypal patterns, universal formative principals. All names for the same reality.

The planets in the signs serve as stimuli in the energy field of the signs. In ancient terms the planets symbolize the gods which must be worshipped. This means that these fundamental life forces cannot be ignored except at the peril of the individual. They must be recognized, paid due attention, and accepted; then the energy inherent in them can be consciously directed. If we are not aware of these forces in our lives, then we are at the mercy of them.

The Greeks felt the great sin was when an individual had the audacity and foolish pride to ignore the gods in some way. Naturally, the gods' nemesis - explosion of pent-up forces that were refused a proper channel - followed inevitably.

Understanding the elements and modalities is the basic foundation of understanding astrology.

Many cultures have included the four elements in their philosophies and mythological traditions.

Your chart shows your energy field or what clairvoyants call the aura.

When we say "someone is out of their element" from the standpoint of astrology, that is probably true - someone is dealing with a realm of activity which is alien to his true nature.

We recharge our batteries by involving ourselves in activities that supply us with the necessary fuel. Signs in different elements would recharge in different ways.

The four elements and the three modalities are discussed in great depth as an education for the practicing astrologer. The remaining chapters of the book are also designed to be used as a reference tool for astrologers.

This has been a very high level overview. Hopefully it will provide useful information concerning the basic energetic philosophy upon which astrology is based.

Cave and Cosmos

Cave and Cosmos, Shamanic Encounters with Another Reality by Michael Harner provides clear insight into the world of shamanism. In the following overview are a few more pieces of the puzzle.

Michael Harner received his doctorate in anthropology in 1963 from the University of California, Berkley. In 1980 he wrote *The Way of the Shaman* which started a worldwide shamanic revival.

In the 1960s psychedelics where *in*. Most of the big universities had programs studying the effects of various consciousness altering substances. Michael Harner discovered shamans in many cultures used drumming as a way to alter consciousness in much the same way some cultures used mind altering substances. He published a drumming CD and taught us how to journey to the underworld without psychedelics.

His new book, *Cave and Cosmos*, is a history of the anthropological study of shamanism and somewhat of psychedelics. He presents many stories recounting the experiences of ordinary people who have taken shamanic journeys. Here you will find instructions on how to journey to the underworld to retrieve your power animal and how to journey to the upper world to meet and seek the help of guides or spirit helpers.

Shamanism in its various forms is an ancient healing modality. Shamans assume humans are a part of the totality of nature, related to all other biological forms and not superior to them. This pagan view is one of the reasons the church persecuted shamans during the Inquisition.

Shamans believe there are two realities and that the perception of each depends on your state of consciousness. The ordinary state of consciousness and the shamanic state of consciousness. In the shamanic state you can access nonordinary reality. A shaman can move back and forth between these two realities at will in order to heal and help others.

The shaman encounters spirits in nonordinary reality. He experiences them as real as his fellow humans.

Living members of all species including humans have souls or personal spirits - present in each of us from conception to death - to varying degrees. At death, the soul continues to exist, as it did before birth, but the length of time it exists varies. Shamans encounter souls in nonordinary reality.

The Universe is divided into three worlds. The Middle World where we live. The Upper World and the Lower World are purely spiritual and are found only in non-ordinary reality where they exist outside of time. The shaman makes out of body journeys to these worlds to seek assistance for healing from compassionate beings there.

Poor health, illness and serious injury are usually due to specific spiritual and nonspiritual factors - the task of the shaman is to deal with the spiritual factors. The spiritual factors are of two types: (1) those that involve a loss by the patient of a spirit important to the patient's well being; (2) the acquisition by the patient of a spirit detrimental to the patient's well being.

In healing a patient a shaman will consult their helping spirits and/or will be able to "see" the spiritual cause of the illness.

Shamans generally believe in a holistic approach to healing and will augment other healing modalities. They often view Western medicine as being concerned primarily with symptom relief rather than true healing at the spirit level.

Shamans only engage in healing at the request of a patient.

Shamanism is the path of independence leading toward spiritual freedom - freedom to know, not just to believe. *Cave and Cosmos* gives the tools to seek help from another reality where teachers and wise and caring spirits are forever ready to heal and share their knowledge, wisdom and compassion.

Maybe the best gift of shamanism is to liberate us from our bindings of belief and disbelief. Now we have a means for direct experience of the non-ordinary. We are no longer restricted to the teachings of heavenly books brought to us by the ancient few. Now we can travel to the origins of the teachings themselves.

For ordinary people who do not aspire to become a shaman, journeying can be very beneficial in self-healing and self awareness. It is safe and involves listening to drumming music which is holding a steady rhythm of 205 to 220 beats per minute.

A shamanic journey is very similar to meditation. The difference is you are journeying for a purpose - one which you decide upon before your journey begins. Several drumming CDs are available - be sure to find one designed for shamanic journeying. Michael Harner has been teaching shamanism for many years. I found the instructions for journeying in his books to be very easy to follow.

I've taken several shamanic journeys since reading *The Way of the Shaman* years ago and have come back with very valuable information. Consider giving it a try.

Illumination

Illumination, The Shaman's Way of Healing by Alberto Villoldo, Ph.D. is a fascinating book. I had the privilege to attend one of Villoldo's workshops a few years ago and was moved by his power and gentleness. The following excerpts and overview are only a small portion of this very important wisdom teaching.

All disease has spiritual origins, and illness is manifested through subtle bodies - the energy body, our emotions, our thoughts - and lastly the physical body. For the shamans, physical and emotional challenges provide an opportunity for initiation and spiritual rebirth into a new way of being. If the opportunity for initiation is missed, a second wake-up call might come in the form of an even more serious malady.

Initiation leads to the death of your old self, to rebirth, and to your illumination.

We pass through a series of awakenings and realizations again and again. Illuminations are a part of our developmental journey - we don't discard any of them as we ascend to the higher rungs - we transcend and include.

Illumination is an inherent faculty of the brain, and not just a gift that some higher power bestows upon us. And while indeed it is possible to receive truth and knowledge directly from Spirit through mysterious means, they (the Laika) discovered that they could attain illumination by successfully completing certain initiations into the mysteries of life.

Seven life passages (initiations) we all experience during our lives - birth, manhood or womanhood, first love, marriage, parenthood, sagehood, and death.

Anything short of illumination is not a complete healing. Shamanic healers don't distinguish cancer, diabetes, or heart disease in their cosmology. Conditions are symptoms of a spiritual illness - the loss of a sacred sense of oneness with the universe, and our neglecting our role as participants in Creation.

You must take part in dreaming the world into being as a participant in creation, or else continue repeating the nightmare of history and have to settle for a world that is being dreamed by others.

We must be willing to follow the path of initiation ourselves, as all great teachers have done. Only then can we begin to craft truly healthy, authentic, and original lives. We are able to grow new bodies that age and heal and die gracefully. We are illumined.

The evolutionary journey from matter to mind to soul to spirit - each step of which transcends and includes the step below it - makes me believe that illumination might be an inherent guiding force of nature.

Initiations are inevitable. If you resist initiation, the universe will conspire to bring you face to face with the end of a stage of your life in some other way. Resistance is futile.

Dissecting the past is a trap. The shaman knows that focusing on our wounds will only reinforce them as we begin to believe that the dramatic personal stories - tragic or heroic - that we tell ourselves about our past are who we are today.

Initiation offers us the opportunity to heal our emotions. All the drama and suffering in our lives is brought about by our unhealed emotions, which give rise to our beliefs about how the world works. The shaman understands that whatever beliefs you hold about the nature of reality, the universe will prove you right.

We can solve any difficulty in our lives - from discovering love to achieving peace in our world - if we heal our emotions and then change our beliefs. You must rewire your brain.

Each initiation marks a break with the past. A mythic initiation requires the death of a personal story and an archetypal rebirth into a new and greater personal myth.

With each passage you discover that you do not die, even when you think the heartbreak is going to kill you, or the loss of your youth is going to devastate you. Eventually, your initiation leads to the discovery of peace, generosity, compassion and illumination.

Seven toxic emotions that must be confronted during initiation -- wrath, greed, lust, sloth, envy, gluttony and pride.

When we break free from these deadly emotions and the beliefs they create about scarcity, powerlessness, intimacy, and fear, we discover that although there is violence in the world, we can live free of violence in our home and in our relationships.

We discover that although it is very difficult to change the world, it is not difficult to change our own world.

A rite of initiation allows you to heal through your own power, instead of recruiting others to be bit players in your emotional dramas.

If you do not discover the lessons that toxic emotions have to teach you, you'll end up marrying someone who will make sure you learn them. Until we heal these deadly emotions, we will continue attracting people who share the same emotional wounds and stories we play out.

Seven virtues known as angels during the middle ages - peace, generosity, purity of intent, courage, compassion, temperance and humility.

When you fail to complete one of your initiations, one of the seven deadly emotions begins to stir in primitive regions of your brain.

Illumination has to be accompanied by an experience of symbolic death and rebirth into a new life.

We have developed a marvelous capacity for denial. You are required to face your death (to old beliefs) and discover your courage.

There are two great leaps in awareness that we make during our initiation: *the awakening to our mortality . . . and the awakening to our immortality . . .*

Eventually the seeker symbolically dies to his earthly existence and awakens to his nature as an infinite being at peace with God. We have a sudden sense of unity with all that is and ever was, a tremendous sense of awe and humility, and a dissolving of the ego. We die to the way of the flesh and are born to the way of Spirit.

Witchcraft

Ever wonder whether witches are real or simply fictional characters representing the shadow side of our psyche? I believe the answer is - both.

First, a little history.

The earliest mention of witches dates back to 560 BC - *The Bible*, Exodus - "Thou shalt not suffer a *witch* to live." The word witch in Exodus is a translation of the Hebrew word *kashaph* which comes from the root meaning to whisper. So, in Exodus it most likely meant one who whispers a spell - meant for the people of the time to adhere to their own religion and not be swayed by the teachings of others.

Saint Augustine argued in the early AD 400s that god alone could suspend the normal laws of the universe. He felt it was the error of Pagans to believe in some other divine power than the one god. The church accepted his view and decided *not* to investigate witches.

Pope Innocent III in 1208 attempted to discredit the Cathars - they believed *both* god and satan had supernatural powers - the fight between good and evil begins. The Church attempted to paint the Cathars as devil worshippers.

Thomas Aquinas in 1273 argued the world was full of evil and dangerous demons. He felt these demons, among other things, would take the sperm of men and spread it among women. He felt sex and witchcraft were associated

- demons sought their own pleasure and also lead men into temptation. Did you ever notice the demons most always are leading *men* to temptation? And, the demons most always are *women*?

In the mid 1400s torture inflicted on heretics suspected of magical pacts or demon-driven sexual misconduct lead to alarming confessions. This is when the crime of witchcraft began to take shape.

Pope Innocent VIII in 1484 announced the satanists in Germany were meeting with demons, casting spells that destroyed crops and aborted infants. He ordered a report be prepared of these activities. This resulted in the publication of *Hammer of Witches* which put to rest the old held belief that witches were powerless and replaced it with the new orthodoxy that held Christians had an obligation to hunt down and kill witches. The *Hammer of Witches* told stories of women who would have sex with any convenient demon, kill babies and even steal penises. Over the next 40 years the *Hammer of Witches* was reprinted 13 times and helped to define the crime of witchcraft.

In the mid 1500s mass executions began to appear. In 1515 authorities in Switzerland burned 500 women at the stake. Nine years later in Como, Italy 1,000 were executed. Witch hysteria swept Europe. Most protections under the law were eliminated for those accused of witchcraft. Between the years of 1500 and 1660, as many as 80,000 suspected witches were executed - 80% of whom were women. Germany takes the prize with as many as 26,000 executions during this time.

King James VI of Scotland (later King James I of England) in 1591 authorized the torture of suspected witches. The genesis of this move was rough seas which he and his new wife experienced on their honeymoon and which the ship's captain blamed on witches. He launched one of the greatest witch hunts in history.

The largest witch hunt in French history occurred in 1643 - 1645. However by the end of the 1640s the number of trials began to drop. Holland by 1648 was a tolerant society that had done away with the punishment of witches.

In 1682 England executed its last witch. Across the Atlantic the outbreak of hysteria began in Salem in 1692. The Enlightenment in the late 1680s contributed to the end of witch hunts throughout Europe. It was also taught that the use of torture to force confessions was inhumane and lead to suspect information being gathered.

What is witchcraft anyway?

Witchcraft is the use of magical faculties. This can take many forms depending on the cultural context. The belief in and the practice of magic has been present since the earliest human cultures and continues to have an important religious and medicinal role in many cultures today.

The concept of witchcraft as harmful is often treated as a cultural ideology providing a scapegoat for human misfortune and conduct. As can be seen from the timeline above witchcraft came to be seen as part of a vast diabolical conspiracy of individuals in league with the devil, undermining Christianity.

As an aside, I wonder if anyone has prepared a comprehensive list of all the people the Catholic church has killed in the name of god in an effort to assure its position of power?

Today witchcraft has become a branch of modern paganism, practiced by those following the Wiccan tradition. Most view this as a spiritual path grounded in love and in living close to natural laws.

The Shadow.

In fiction stories witches often represent the dark side of human nature. They can take many forms. Darth Vader in *Star Wars* - the dark side of the force. Agent Smith in *The Matrix*.

The Buddha taught we are born total and complete, lacking nothing. The light *and* the dark - all right in here. Which do I choose to express?

The above historical timeline clearly shows the mass projection of the dark out onto others in the societies of the times. Isn't it amazing the extent to which the people of these times needed a scapegoat so as not to own their own dark side. And, the church was the leader of the pack - all in the name of god. How very sad.

The Lesson.

"Whatever we reject in ourselves, we project onto others. Whatever we disown, owns us. Whatever we resist, persists. By making conscious what has been unconscious, we trans-form; we go beyond our current configuration, into a higher, more unified level of consciousness." - Stephanie Austin, *Mountain Astrologer*, Oct/Nov 2013

Reference: *A Brief History of Witchcraft Persecutions before Salem* by Douglas Linder, 2005

The Wheel of the Year

In Pagan times the Sabbats from the Greek *sabatu* meaning to rest were festivals honoring the growth cycle of crops - planting, tending, harvesting and allowing the land to rest. They celebrated the path of the Sun from high in the sky and warm to low in the sky and cool - the seasons. Many pagans saw time as one eternal whole. The god is born of the eternal goddess, dies, and is reborn. A life well lived was lived in harmony and rhythm with these cycles.

It is thought the Sabbats have been celebrated in many places and in various forms for at least 12,000 years. Some estimate much, much longer. In modern times there are still those who follow the old Pagan ways.

With the advent of christianity and the brutal persecution of any non-christians, the pagans went into hiding which preserved the old ways. Even many christian holy-days are based on these ancient pagan rites.

The pagan year begins in March with the Spring Equinox - Ostara.

Ostara - Spring Equinox - March

The Spring Equinox - Ostara. The days and nights are equal - a magic time - the veils between the worlds are very thin. To some this is considered the true beginning of the New Year. The first day of Spring when the Sun moves from Pisces, the last sign of winter, into Aries, the first sign of Spring. When light again triumphs over darkness.

Consider taking a moment to celebrate Ostara a time of new, powerful, magical beginnings. What is beginning in your life?

Beltane - Cross Quarter Day - May

Beltane is a cross quarter day. It is the mid-point between the spring equinox (Ostara in the olden days) and the summer solstice (Litha in olden times).

At Beltane the Pleiades star cluster rises just before sunrise on the morning horizon. The Pleiades is a cluster of seven closely placed stars, the seven sisters, in the constellation of Taurus, near his shoulder.

Beltane marks the beginning of summer and was a time when cattle were driven out to the summer pastures. Rituals were performed to protect the cattle, crops and people, and to encourage growth. Special bonfires were kindled, and their flames, smoke and ashes were deemed to have protective powers.

Modern holidays tied to these old customs are: May Day, May 1; Cinco de Mayo (Mexico), May 5; and, Mother's Day, the second Sunday in May.

Litha - Summer Solstice - June

Solstice, or Litha, means a stopping or standing still of the sun. It is the longest day of the year and the time when the sun is at its maximum elevation.

This date has had spiritual significance for thousands of years as humans have been amazed by the great power of the sun. The Celts celebrated with bonfires that would add to the sun's energy, Christians placed the feast of St. John the Baptist towards the end of June and it is also the festival of Li, the Chinese Goddess of light.

This is a time to celebrate growth and life. For pagans, who see balance in the world and are deeply aware of the ongoing shifting of the seasons, it is also a time to acknowledge that the sun will now begin to decline once more towards winter.

Midsummer day is marked around the time of the summer solstice but should not be confused with it. European celebrations of Midsummer take place on a day between June 21 and June 24, depending on regional traditions. In the United Kingdom Midsummer day takes place on June 24, the feast of St. John the Baptist.

Lammas - Cross Quarter Day - August

Lammas, also called Lughnasadh, was traditionally a harvest festival day. Originally it was held August 1st, or approximately halfway between the summer solstice and the autumn equinox. However, over time the celebrations shifted to the Sundays nearest this date. It is one of the eight Sabbats in the pagan Wheel of the Year and is the first of three autumn harvest festivals.

Throughout history, Pagan worshippers in Ireland, Britain, and Europe have celebrated their bountiful harvests on this day and offered prayers and sacrifices for the success of future crops.

In olden times on this day it was customary to bake loaves of bread from the first grain harvest and bring them to church to be blessed. In some cultures the loaves might be used afterwards to work Magic. A book of Anglo-Saxon charms directed that the Lammas bread be broken into four bits, which were to be placed at the four corners of the barn, to protect the garnered grain. Some believe the word Lammas is a shortened form of *loaf mass*.

Since many fruits, vegetables, and grains today are available to us year round, this celebration is now somewhat overlooked. The holiday is still important for many around the world as it marks the end of summer and the welcoming of autumn.

Mabon - Autumn Equinox - September

The Autumn Equinox divides the day and night equally. We give thanks to the warm light of the summer and the crops that have been grown and stored for the winter to come. The brilliant fall colors begin to show and we sense the cyclical time of rest that is to come. It is a time to finish old business as we ready for a period of rest, relaxation, and reflection.

At the same time, we honor the dark. From the moment of the September Equinox, the Sun's strength diminishes. The days become shorter until the moment of the Winter Solstice in December, when the Sun again grows stronger and the days once again become longer than the nights. Cycles upon cycles in an endless dance.

In the pagan tradition Mabon is the mid-harvest festival, and it is when we take a few moments to honor the changing seasons, and celebrate the second harvest. The Druids call this celebration, Mea'n Fo'mhair, and honor the Green Man, the God of the Forest, by offering libations to trees. Offerings of ciders, wines, herbs and fertilizer are appropriate at this time.

Wiccans celebrate the aging Goddess as she passes from Mother to Crone, and her consort the God as he prepares for death and re-birth.

Samhain - Cross Quarter Day - October

Samhain - summer's end - is a Gaelic festival marking the end of the harvest season and the beginning of winter or the darker half of the year. It is celebrated from sunset on October 31 to sunset on November 1, which is nearly halfway between the autumn equinox and the winter solstice.

Samhain is mentioned in some of the earliest Irish literature and is known to have pre-Christian roots. Many important events in Irish mythology happen or begin on Samhain. It was the time when cattle were brought back down from the summer pastures and when livestock were slaughtered for the winter. Herbs were gathered one last time and dried.

As at Beltane, special bonfires were lit. These were deemed to have protective and cleansing powers and there were rituals involving them. Samhain (like Beltane) was seen as a time when the veil between life and death grows thin and spirits or fairies could more easily come into our world.

In the 9th century, the Roman Catholic Church shifted the date of All Saints Day to November 1, while November 2 later became All Souls Day. Over time, Samhain and All Saints/All Souls merged and helped to create the modern Halloween. Historians used the name Samhain to refer to Gaelic Halloween customs up until the 19th century.

Samhain is celebrated as the Dia de los Muertos in Mexico - the Day of the Dead - usually on November 1. Some churches fix November 7 as All Hallows Eve. Some fix November 11 as Martinmas - when the sun reaches the actual cross quarter day in Scorpio.

Yule - Winter Solstice - December

The Winter Solstice is the shortest day of the year and the official beginning of winter in the northern hemisphere. Christmas - the birth of Jesus Christ - is now celebrated on December 25. It was originally set at this time of the year to coincide with the pagan solstice or Yule celebrations. The solstice can occur on different days each year. The actual date of the birth of Jesus Christ is not known. It has been speculated to be in the Spring of the year.

In the pagan traditions at Yule or Yuletide the God, who died at Samhain, is reborn of the *Virgin* Goddess. The God is represented by the sun which returns after this darkest night to again bring warmth to the land.

Lights on houses and trees are a modern version of the pagan custom of lighting candles and fires as acts of magic to lure back the waning sun. Today it is still a custom in Ireland and Norway to leave lights burning all through the house on Yule night to not only lure back the sun, but also to honor the Virgin Goddess who gives him birth.

Interestingly enough, the word "virgin" is one which was mistranslated and misrepresented by the early Church, enough to make even people today forget that the term had absolutely nothing to do with the hymen. The term "virgin" was first applied to priestesses in Mediterranean temples, particularly during Rome's Pagan period. The term identified a woman who was a complete entity unto herself, who was not bound by secular law, had no husband and was free to take all the lovers she chose. She needed nothing else and no one else for completeness. In other words she was said to be "intact" - a virgin.

The word Yule comes from the Old Norse traditions and means wheel and was often referred to as the turning time. In the Norse tradition Yule was a twelve night long celebration.

Wreaths have been used in a symbolic way for more than 4,000 years. The wreath's circle has no beginning and no end, illustrating the Wheel of the Year is also like this with everything in time coming back to its point of origin and traveling onward, over and over again. Pinecones in wreaths represent male fertility and fruit such as apples represent the Goddess and female fertility.

Many, many modern customs at this time of year have their origin in old pagan traditions from the various cultures.

Imbolg - Cross Quarter Day - February

Imbolg is a cross quarter day. It is also known as Candlemas or Brigid's Day and is one of four Celtic Fire Festivals. Winter for our pagan ancestors was a harsh season, one during which many died of disease and malnutrition. This celebration was designed to lure back the Sun and speed up the coming signs of Spring.

In Ireland this was a holy day for honoring the Great Mother Goddess, Brigid, in her guise as the waiting bride of the youthful Sun God who was now returning to her. Her festival was so important even the church was pressured into naming a holiday after her - St. Bridget's Day - even though in reality they are honoring the Goddess.

The return of the Sun and the very early, first signs of Spring are celebrated. Look around for the first sprouting of leaves or the Crocus flowers. Winter has passed and signs of new life are appearing. The agricultural year which brings nourishment will return soon at Ostara, the Spring Equinox in March.

This Sabbat was once celebrated with fire - torches, bonfires, fire in every form. Maidens wore a crown of lighted candles. Fire here represents our own illumination and inspiration. This is a festival of light and fertility.

This festival also marks the transition point of the threefold Goddess energies from those of Crone to Maiden - and the wheel turns.

Reference: *Sabbats* by Edain McCoy, 2011

Tarot - The Wonder of Being

"The first and foremost essential service of a mythology is this one, of opening the mind and heart to the utter wonder of being." - Joseph Campbell

The Tarot is a deck of cards with symbols on them. I expect over the ages there have been hundreds or thousands of different Tarot decks produced. No one really knows where the Tarot originated. It is associated with gypsies, an old English abbreviation of Egyptian.

Playing cards, generally, are thought to have originated in China and Korea, some think India. Some date the cards to AD 600, others earlier. No one knows where or when the symbols on the cards originated. The first appearance of Tarot cards in the West was in Europe in the 14th century. Christianity reigned supreme, but paganism was still alive and well. There were many heretical Christian sects back then, today loosely grouped under *Gnostic*. In Greek the word means someone who knows, a wise person, an initiate - and, some believe, wizard or witch.

The cards are used as an oracle, much in the same way as the I-Ching in the East. The Tarot is based on symbols - a universal language where our inner and outer worlds can communicate. Carl Jung said: "the psychological mechanism for transforming energy is the symbol." When you work with the Tarot deck you will find the symbols themselves evoke memories, associations, inspiration, clarification and validation for your current issues, goals and choices.

The Tarot is a symbolic map of consciousness expressed in symbols. The 78 symbols represent archetypes of inner and outer human experiences. Working with the Tarot can help you get in tune with your intuition and can be used for personal growth and development. You begin a dialog with the unseen. In my personal case, a dialog that has been on-going for many years. Sounds crazy, but it's not. Just like astrology, it's very real.

If you choose to give working with the Tarot a try, remember to use the symbols as keys or creative ideas that can help to unlock connections or associations which will enable you to penetrate deeper into the mystery of life. A simple way to use the Tarot is as an oracle. If you are confused or would like guidance, sincerely ask that you be given helpful information by the card you choose from the deck. You might be surprised how right on the information may be.

As I said earlier, there are lots of Tarot decks for sale these days. The one I have used for many, many years is Aleister Crowley *Thoth Tarot*. This deck contains cross-cultural Egyptian, Grecian, Eastern, Medieval and Christian symbolism. It also incorporates numerology, astrology, alchemy and the Cabala. Each card was painted by Lady Frieda Harris under the direction of Aleister Crowley. The project spanned five years, between 1938 and 1943. I love the symbols and art of this deck. Although, I didn't enjoy the book written by Aleister Crowley to go with it. The book I use for interpretation is *Tarot, The Handbook* by Angeles Arrien.

Consider opening your mind to the unknown and to your own innate intuition.

I Ching - the Book of Changes

We have had a spiritual revival in the West dating back to the 1960s, maybe before. Ideas from the East - Buddhism, primarily - ideas of acceptance, of being part of all existence, without posing values and making judgments - were brought to the West by pioneers during this time. The idea of oneness, a basic unity among all things was the foundation of these new ideas. The Taoists of ancient China, formulators of the I Ching, called it the Tao or the Way.

This idea has made its way into the culture of the West. New generations have a more neutral, less ambitious and less neurotic attitude toward the material world. Or, I hope they do.

The Tao or the Way is a gateway through which we are constantly passing. We are never before the gate nor beyond it. Nothing exists except there, with us, at that moment, *in* the gateway. We are always on the path, on the Way, even if we don't know we are.

The Yin and Yang symbols reflect the constantly changing, dying and rejuvenating universe more perfectly than does Darwin's theory of survival. By discovering these deeper meanings for ourselves, we discover more of the totality of experience. This is the secret behind all systems of magic or divination. The Tarot, astrology and the I Ching are each a microcosm of the range of human experience.

Hesitation, anxiety, dissatisfaction are to the Taoist what sin is to the Christian. To dispel them and to clear the mind of confusion, the I Ching is devoutly cast. The resulting hexagram indicates to the questioner his Tao, his Way, his natural direction with regard to the problem he is facing.

The belief is that just as the question is a part of you the answer you seek is part of you. With the help of the I Ching you can bring forth the answer you already possess.

A bundle of 50 sticks is used. Yarrow sticks cut the same length are traditional for the oracle. Sometimes coins are used. The casting of the sticks or throwing of the coins is not thought to be magic, only a mechanical means whereby the pattern of the forces that shape the Tao can be determined. It takes between half an hour and an hour to cast off the yarrow sticks. There is much time for meditation during this time.

The result will be 64 hexagrams - 64 examples of different ways of life that cover the entire range of human experience. Through interpretation of the hexagrams, the Way is revealed to the questioner.

There are many books explaining the method of casting the sticks or coins, how to record the resulting hexagrams and how to interpret the results. The *I Ching or Book of Changes (Bollingen Series General)*, Hellmut Wilhelm, C. G. Jung, Richard Wilhelm, Cary F. Baynes is a great book for the serious seeker. A lighter weight version is *The I Ching or Book of Changes* by Brian Browne Walker.

Working with the I Ching, like the Tarot or astrology has the potential to open you to your own innate intuition and wisdom. You might consider giving it a try?

Final Thoughts

Well, there you have it. Lots of pieces for the puzzle of life. Some of what you read, hopefully, will help you on your way. I've included excerpts and overviews of many books. To me, really important books discussing new ideas or old wisdom in a way that is accessible to us today. Some of it is "out there" for most people living in the West. I believe it's humanity's direction.

My intention in writing about wisdom, as I see it, is to shake up your world - maybe help you see what is known and what is unknown in a new way. And, mostly, to help you see yourself more clearly - and life.

I hope you will consider - you *are* love - limitless, unconditional love. Nothing to do, no trying. You simply have to be the wonderful, magical person you already are. Cool, right?

Once we can all live in that place, peace can't be too far behind.

Remember: "We are all just walking each other home." Thank you, Ram Dass, for that wisdom.

I wish you well on your journey.

Ann Ranson, 2014

Discovering Wisdom
When We Realize We Are Love - Everything Shifts

INDEX

Discovering Wisdom
When We Realize We Are Love - Everything Shifts

Discovering Wisdom
When We Realize We Are Love - Everything Shifts

15216138R10156

Made in the USA
San Bernardino, CA
18 September 2014